# TREASURE FOUND

# treasure found

## A GIFT FROM MY
## INNER CHILD TO YOURS

LANA WILLIAMS

Lana Williams/Look With Me, LLC
www.lookwithmecoaching.com
Ordering information: Special discounts are available on quantity purchases by corporations,
associations, and others. For details, contact the author at this email address:
*** lana@lookwithmecoaching.com

Paperback ISBN: 978-1-7363028-0-4
eBook ISBN: 978-1-7363028-1-1
Hardcover ISBN: 978-1-7363028-2-8

# DISCLAIMER

*The intent of this book is to offer information of a general nature to help you on your quest for a joyful, healthy, and fulfilled life. The author of this book does not dispense medical or psychological advice to the individual reader. This book is not intended as a substitute form of treatment or as a replacement for receiving consultation and advice from your physician or therapist. In the event you use any of the information in this book for yourself, it would be understood that you fully own and are responsible for your personal choices and actions and that the author and publisher assume no responsibility for those choices and actions.*

*The views and opinions expressed in this book concerning any institutions are those of the author and do not necessarily reflect the position of those institutions or of her fellow graduates and colleagues. The author is very proud to be an alumnus of all of her training institutions and considers the experiences and education received as highly valuable and a privilege.*

*The people mentioned within this book are real, but names and identifying facts may have been changed out of respect of privacy. They are all considered by the author to be beautiful, well intended, good people who, like her, were doing the best they could considering their conditioning and current awareness at that time. Nothing in this book was written by the author with an intent to cause harm or paint anyone in a negative light. Those mentioned in this book would be expected to have their own interpretations and perspectives when they recall the events for themselves and may or may not recall those experiences in the same way. The author intentionally chose to only include the stories and/or experiences that most significantly impacted her journey toward learning how to love herself unconditionally.*

# DEDICATION

*To the child within you.*

*To Dad, whose heart was more beautiful than he allowed himself to acknowledge: Doing the best he knew how with the conditioning he was given, he raised daughters by himself in spite of the odds against him. My heart is saddened from missing your smile, but it's also full of gratitude and celebration for you. Rest now in peace.*

# CONTENTS

# ACKNOWLEDGMENTS

Thank you to my soul partner and husband. I'm in love with every moment of our journey together.

Thank you to Dad who raised his daughters in the midst of what I can only imagine must have been a very trying time in his life; he still showed up for us every day. Dad, I love you fully and unconditionally.

Thank you to the Institute of Professional Excellence in Coaching (iPEC) for your coach training and for your mission "to raise the consciousness of the world, one person at a time."

Thank you to Morgan Field for paving the way for what's possible as a coach and "soul-preneur." I see your magical and powerful inner little one as such a fun, unstoppable force! Thank you for creating the Epic Book Writing Group and bringing together our soul book writing tribe (J, J, and T). This group was the formal invitation and the beautiful safe space that I needed to help me birth my first "book baby." Thank you, ladies, for showing up so raw and powerful and beautiful each week!

Thank you to my editor, Stephanie Gunning, and book designer, Danna of Dearly Creative, for lending your energy and expertise to help me polish and package this gem.

I am deeply grateful to the people portrayed in this book for their priceless and significant roles in my journey to self-love.

Their memories of the events described in this book may be very different than my own, but I truly believe had it not been for everyone mentioned in this book, I would not have found the joy and love for myself that I have today. To my knowledge, some good has come from all of the stories described, even if it was not apparent at the time.

Thank you, Spirit, for using little Lou to show me that even tragedy can be part of a bigger beautiful picture when my heart is open and I rise to look from a higher view.

# INTRODUCTION

What if you could live with the confidence and security of knowing that someone would always be there to take care of you? Someone would always have your back?

What if you knew that even if you failed, there would be a place for you to return full of love and safety?

What if you were certain someone would be there to hold you as you cried, nurse your wounds as long as needed, and until you were ready to try again?

**Would you live your life differently if you knew mistakes and failures, judgments and criticisms, didn't actually matter?**

To have support, safety, and confidence would've been an absolute dream for me as a child, but that wasn't the case. Instead, my world often felt very unsafe. I grew up feeling fragile and insecure, although it might not have seemed so to an onlooker. I was the class president at my high school, graduating fourth in my class and with honors. I broke records as a student-athlete, earning both an academic scholarship and an athletic scholarship that together paid for my university education. I went on to medical school and became a physician with a six-figure income. I was rarely without a handsome boyfriend in tow. Throughout, I was a daddy's girl, and my younger sister often found herself lost in my shadow. My entire adult world was set up to protect me from the awful truth hidden at my core.

My truth was that on an otherwise ordinary night in September, during my seventh year of life, the little girl version of me witnessed my mother's choice to end her life abruptly and leave her two daughters and husband behind. After that night, this child spent the next thirty-plus years dedicating her total energy and actions to being as good, hardworking, obedient, and responsible as she could be so that she would have a chance of having her dream come true of finding a loving, safe place to live that she could call home. What the little girl inside me never realized was that the entire time she was doing each of the things she did to succeed and be happy, she was desperately running away from the very real, very deep pain of feeling abandoned and alone. She was running away from the pain born on that traumatic night in September.

That little girl's answers finally came when she stopped running. That child, now living in my adult body, would like to present her story to you. She wants to share it with you in the hope that it will help you recognize that you are not alone.

And yes, the phrase *you are not alone* is a cliché. It sounds like that to me as well. It is a thing that people are inclined to say when they try to make the lonely feel better. It seemed so overused that even as I'd watch someone speak those words to me, I'd wonder if they knew it wasn't making any sense to me, because I most certainly did feel alone.

And yet here I am, like countless people before me, having ultimately learned that even in our darkest hours we aren't alone.

Here's what my little girl and I know now. We've acquired knowledge from multiple sources, including doctors, psychotherapists, life coaches, and spiritual teachers, as well as through the unadulterated education of pure life experience, that confirms there comes a time when our young selves have to make sense of the world around us and of the pain that may have been inflicted on us.

As children, we do our best to conform to and play the roles being demanded of us so that we may stay safe, fit in, and be loved. You've probably heard this so many times before, but it's worth repeating. We learn the hurtful truth that it's not enough just to be who we are. Period. To protect ourselves from further hurt, shame, or judgment, or, as in my case, to defend against further abandonment, we adopt our parents' and community's judgmental ideas as our own. We identify with, or assume the identity of, the persona that our inner and outer worlds tell us we should embody in order to be OK in any given situation.

For children, being so small and without seeing the full picture, the protective identities we take on can consume us to the degree that we forget who we are. Even in the best of homes, this conforming, suppressing, and adopting of new identities will inevitably happen because of our schools, or our society's, or our religion's, or our friend's, or our partner's influence, which is layered over our own desires to be safe, to be approved of, and to be loved. But by taking on these protective personas, we abandon ourselves.

Thankfully, I have now learned that this is all just a part of life's amazing journey. What I also ultimately learned is this:

When I came home to my authenticity, to the essence of who I am without all those assumed identities, I opened a portal to abundant love. I opened the door to a joyful, love-filled life. And with each sunrise, I can walk through that door with a smile on my face, knowing I am choosing love. I am choosing to be the fullest and brightest expression of myself I can be in that moment. It's always been my choice.

Am I choosing to experience love and connection today? Am I choosing to experience growth, raise my consciousness, and be a contributing part of someone else's expansion today? Am I choosing to experience the freedom to play and be light today?

Or am I choosing to live as if on autopilot, abandoning myself and going through the motions, but missing out on it all?

At the end of the book, I'll share a summary with you of many of my light bulb moments and describe the practices I now use each day to remind me that it's up to me to choose **how** I wish to experience my life's journey.

Sprinkled throughout, I've also marked pages with a few diamonds and pearls, statements that are compassionate reminders of the many hidden gems that were there for me along the way, even if I didn't notice them at the time. When you see a **DIAMOND** or a **PEARL** icon, please pause to reread the statement or to write it down in your journal before you go on. The hope would be that if those parts of my story resonate as familiar to the little one inside of you, you can learn to spot those gems in your own life sooner than I did.

I feel inspired by my own journey and excited to share part of it with you. My little one was first abandoned by her own mother. She was then abandoned by me over and over again. But once I discovered her, and saw how bright and truly amazing she is, everything changed. My little one has now experienced the beautiful, hot alchemy of melting cares. She's felt big arms open to her and say, "Come to me, I'm here for you," and she nestled right into them, as she would when she was cuddling her beloved dog. My little one now believes that we are ALL meant to be nurtured and allowed to fully blossom under the radiant light of unconditional love.

This book is an offering from the child inside of me to the little one inside of you. I invite you to read about my personal journey of abandonment and of feeling discarded for not being worthy, and discover how I finally came to experience full-on unconditional love. If you've ever found yourself asking, "When will deep and unshakeable, heart-centered love be there for me?" or "When will it be my turn to wake up and be at peace, knowing life is on my side and love is always there?" Or if you simply like to read inspirational stories that remind you of how, at some level, we're all on the same journey and never alone, then this book was written for you.

From my heart to yours.

# EXPECTATIONS AND
# REQUESTS FOR THE READER

What should you expect from reading this book?

1. **Excitement or elation.** The stories and light bulbs of **DIAMONDS** and **PEARLS** you'll discover were intended to be exciting! You can expect feelings of lightness in anticipation of what's possible. Your little one will likely jump around inside of you in celebration at the prospect of you seeing and reconnecting with it!

2. **Transient discomfort.** What may potentially also follow the aforementioned light bulb moments and increased awareness are feelings of discomfort. You may find yourself feeling irritable or sad. You may want to lash out at someone out of nowhere. This type of response comes from not being able to unsee painful patterns once you've seen them. Please remember, discomfort is normal for someone who is finally giving permission to the little one inside her to feel and use its voice. This type of reaction could happen within minutes of reading a story that resonates with you or it might happen during the following weeks.

*NOTE:* If intense and uncomfortable emotions arise that are not transient, but stick around, please seek appropriate support from a mental health counselor or doctor. My mom was suffering from chronic depression, which was painful to the point that she believed her only choice was to take her own life. She did not get the help she needed.[1] And even though I am often speaking to you in this book from a child's perspective, the topic of depression and thoughts of suicide are by no means taken lightly here.

3. **Opportunities.** Look out for and anticipate opportunities to arise *coincidentally.* Be prepared for odd and unpredictable *positive* changes to your perfectly laid-out plans. As I aligned with my little one, splendid *coincidences* started to occur and perfectly timed opportunities were presented to me that led me to feel light, joyful, free, and supported.

If any of these three expectations above seem overwhelming, especially if it triggers you to feel an intense fear of change, I recommend that you honor your hesitation and do not read this book. At least not right now. This book is a gift to your inner little one, and I would expect that your little one will almost certainly have more gifts to return to you, gifts that will almost positively include change!

Before you read further, I would make the following requests of you.

---

1 National Suicide Prevention Lifeline, https://suicidepreventionlifeline.org.

1. **Have compassion and patience with yourself.** As we discover patterns in ourselves that may have kept us living blindly and on autopilot (possibly for years), we benefit greatly from self-compassion. What that looks like is acceptance that we could not have known what we didn't yet know. We're really only ready to hear and change when we're really ready…and not any sooner.

2. **Consider that your patterns/behaviors are bringing you some form of secondary gain.** We always gain "something" from our choices even if that thing is hidden and not obvious. Even if it doesn't make sense, we can trust that somewhere inside us we once believed the behaviors we relied on were in our own best interest. There's no shame in that at all.

# PART ONE

*motherless child*

# CHAPTER 1

# *That Night*

I'm thinking we should go for it and jump in the deep end together, as this will force us to get acquainted right away. Besides, I doubt I can hold this child back much longer. She's really excited to tell you a few of the stories she's kept hidden. She has a loud voice now, and she no longer lets the fear of rejection stop her. Basically, she's ready to talk and talk and talk.

It's kind of funny now to remember how much I loved to talk when I was young, although it was usually deterred. I'd have Dad's attention for a brief moment here and there and couldn't wait to share the day's events with him, so I made sure to include all the details. He'd laugh and tell people about how I talked too much. I recall even talking to strangers—obviously before I learned from my dad how scary the world was supposed to be.

My reputation for "running my mouth," as Dad would describe it, stayed with me all the way to medical school. He once gave me his version of a pep talk before I started my clinical rotations. It sounded like this: "Now you know you'll be with *doctors* [emphasis on that word was intended to convey a clear visual image of old white men in white coats acting very serious and intellectual], so remember to keep your mouth shut and just listen. You know how you can get."

The underlying message was that the "little mixed-race girl in the white man's world should stay quiet, learn what she can, and hopefully sneak through under the radar unscathed."

Well, today there's no longer a need for her to sneak under the radar and I'm happy to let you hear her speak. Please allow me to introduce you to my little girl. I've nicknamed her Lou. Her birth certificate carries the name Lana Jean. *Lana* after her mom, *Jean* after her paternal aunt. But once she and I became acquainted, we both preferred for her to have her own name. There will be no more living someone else's story.

I chose the name Lou because two of my absolute favorite people, who were the first ones to really see me and love what they saw, both *coincidentally* happened to nickname me Lou. One of them endearingly started calling me Lana Lou out of the blue. She thought it was cute, so she'd giggle when she'd say it. The other had a handful of nicknames for me, but his favorite was Bubs, which became Bubby, then Bubbalou—finally resting on Lou, for short.

I have looked up the meanings of these names. The name *Lana* in ancient Greek meant "bright one" or "shining one." In other languages, it means "light" or "child." Lou means "warrior" in ancient Greek. But in some other languages, it means "flowery blossom" and "God was gracious."

I can see that my Lou was a warrior, alright; she often engaged in ongoing internal conflict even if not with the world. All that she'd experienced in her young life still surprises me sometimes. But Lou's light has also helped me shine bright, blossom, and feel grateful for the magnificence of life itself.

You'll see.

It's time to let Lou tell you her story. She's been patiently waiting. And just for clarity, I'll delineate when Lou is speaking compared to me when I ask her questions. In case you're confused, just remember they are both me.

*I've just learned to listen to myself better.*

OK. Without further ado, here's Lou.

Me: Hey, sweetie, what's important to you about telling the story about that night?

Lou: Little ones need to know that they're OK. And that it feels good to be heard. Reminds me what I'm made of.

Me: Thank you. Please share what you remember about that night. It's OK. It's your time.

Lou: I remember Dad on the phone waving Mom away, waving for her to get out of the room as if he didn't want her near him while he talked. Mom then escorted me to bed. Her hands rested on my shoulders as she walked me down the hall toward our bedroom and away from the kitchen. I could sense her anger and could feel something wasn't right. So, when she left me in the bedroom, I didn't go right to sleep.

Me: What did you do?

Lou: I watched her through the partly cracked, open door. Our room was dark, but the hall was bright. I could see the back of her as she walked back toward the kitchen. I always was in awe of how tall she was and of her long, thick, brown hair extending most of the way down her back. As I watched her disappear down the hallway, I held my breath and braced myself for what might happen next. But nothing happened; no noise, no arguing, not much of anything. Then, I fell asleep.

Me: So, what happened?

Lou: I was woken by my dog's crying—that kind of doggie whine or whimpering they make when they're sad. She was pacing across my legs on the bed. I petted her thick, soft, wavy, fluffy fur (she was an Old English sheepdog) as I gazed out of the window into the night. My bed was set up beneath a window facing the backyard so I could easily see the entire yard without needing to sit up.

On the left, the backyard was lined by tall trees, planted closely together like a fence for the sake of privacy. There was a peach tree in the back, and on the right, a vegetable garden running along the fence, which had grape vines peeking in and out of it. But none of that was visible that night. All I could see was the open space of the backyard, dimly lit by the night sky. Then, right there in the middle, I saw her lying still and flat on the ground. She was twisted into a weird position, with the long gun that my parents kept under their bed by her side. I'm not sure how long I stared out into the night at her body, but I already sensed there would be no movement. I was sure something terrible had happened, although I wasn't exactly sure what.

Me: What did you feel when you saw her?

Lou: Nothing. Or maybe *empty* is a better word. I think I also felt a little relief. I just pulled the covers over me, held my dog, and went back to sleep.

Me: Relief? And why didn't you get up?

Lou: Sooo much, too much, was going on between them all of the time. Relief that it might end now.

Me: You tell the story so calmly. Weren't there any other feelings?

Lou: *Empty* is the best word I have. I don't really have words to describe the actual feeling. But I can say that I didn't stay asleep. I woke up again, but this time from hearing Dad crying under my window out in the backyard. Blue and red lights were flashing in the distance. She was gone.

I called out to Dad and asked him what was wrong. I didn't tell him I knew. I think I wanted him to tell me the truth and volunteer some answers or explanations for what was going on in our home. But he didn't. He only replied that he had twisted his ankle and said for me to go back to sleep. That confirmed it. She really was gone, and so I tried to stay quiet and went back to sleep as I was told.

Me: I'm still stuck on the absence of feeling. Were there any new feelings by then?

Lou: Maybe a little sadness for Dad since, from what I knew, he never cried. He was a tough ex-professional football player and I don't remember ever having seen him cry before that night. But soon I did feel a little anger creep in, too. I remember thinking, *Mom did this to hurt him.* The anger was also because I wasn't surprised by his lie; and because I was noticing that I, too, was now lying by not telling him I saw her earlier.

Me: Yes, I can remember despising dishonesty, too. And earlier you referred to yourself as trying to stay quiet. Please tell me more about that.

Lou: In our house, I somehow always knew it was better to stay quiet and just to watch and listen. Don't talk too much, don't talk back. Quiet obedience was safest.

Me: It sounds like quietly watching, listening, picking up subtle cues like facial expressions, gestures, inflections, and tone of voice, and sensing the energy in the room, were your superpowers. It makes perfect sense that in a volatile environment these activities would keep you safe.

Lou: Yes! I know they're your superpowers, too: listening and sensing energy.

Me: Ha! Yep! I can also shift energy now, too! But is there more you'd like to share with our readers about that night?

Lou: Not about that night, but about the next morning. I must've slept through the rest of the night as this is the next thing I remember. Dad called my sister and me into his room. Dad said to us, "Your mother decided to go visit her parents earlier than planned." (They both had been telling us recently that she would be leaving to spend some time with her parents.)

*Really, Dad? Another lie?* was all I could think.

But this time, to my surprise, he stopped himself mid-sentence, shook his head, and finally said, "No, sit down. Your mother is gone, and she's not coming back. She's died."

I don't remember if these were really his exact words because my sister let out the most gut-wrenching cry I have ever heard while he was speaking. And her crying didn't stop. I watched as she wailed while Dad held her. I cried a little at seeing her so sad. She'd always been inseparable from Mom. For instance, if a stranger would try to talk to us while we were on a walk, my sister would bury her face in Mom's legs and cling to her like she was hugging a tree trunk.

Meanwhile, as I mentioned before, I would be fine chatting up a stranger. I think I was jealous of my sister's closeness to Mom. But most of my memories of being close to Mom are of sitting next to her while she cried. Mom cried a lot. I would touch her head to see if I could help her, but it never worked.

Me: Was there anything else you noticed as you watched your sister cry and heard the news from Dad?

Lou: I had a thought that I needed to help her now, my sister. But it's tough to explain what that felt like. The feeling was somewhere in my chest and head.

Me: Anything else you'd like to say?

Lou: I loved my dog. Thank you, Yaro [our family dog's name]. You were an angel to me.

Me: Thank you for sharing, Little Lou. Love you.

# CHAPTER 2

# Abandoned Once, Abandoned Twice

To have the confidence of feeling supported, safe, and uncon-ditionally loved would've been an absolute dream for me as a child. This is not to say that my parents didn't intend for me to feel those things; only that I didn't. As a child (and who am I kidding?—as an adult, too), I would imagine that there must have been homes out there where the moms were the open-arms, nurturing types and the dads displayed a perfect mix of strength and gentleness. I guessed that if you were a child in such a home, you could explore the world, make mistakes, and try again, knowing that your parents had your back no matter what.

I would imagine there were children out there with parents who asked them questions like: "What kinds of things excite you or make you the happiest?" "What do you want to do when you grow up, and how can I help make that happen for you?"

Or parents who'd remind their kids, if they happened to change their minds and find something else that suited them better, "It's perfectly all right to shift gears," and "It'll be fun to explore that, too!"

I hoped a home like that existed somewhere, but that was not my reality as a child. In our house, my sister and I were taught that the world is scary. Volatility and aggression were the way to handle disputes and your discomfort. And since the scary world required you to have a lot of money to keep you safe (money that we certainly didn't have), the best way to barely scrape by was through hard work and sacrifice, probably doing something you only kind of liked—or, more accurately, something that you had to learn to like.

In my world, very few places felt safe. My go-tos for comfort were snuggling on the floor with my dog or hiding under the bed with my teddy bear.

Often, I found refuge at Sunday school, where they taught us that God loves everyone, especially children. That felt really good—until I no longer was a child. The adults would continually remind us of the ways we should act and talk and think to ensure we stayed in His good graces. Especially being obedient. So, in full pursuit of the dream of feeling loved and safe in this scary world, I got really good at this obedience thing. I'd do whatever it took to get anywhere close to believing someone, anyone, had my back; and I made sure I was in everyone's good graces, especially God's and Dad's.

You'd think this book would tell you that being an ever-obedient, responsible daughter worked out for me. It didn't. No matter how well I mastered obedience and attempting to keep myself safe from harm, it seemed like harm came knocking on my door anyway.

I've already introduced you to Little Lou (little me), a nonstop-talking, singing, dancing, drawing, reading, exploring, animal-whispering, skinny little biracial girl. I was pretty happy in general as a young kid, and initially, I had no idea the world was a place I should be afraid of, until my seventh year. For reasons I couldn't explain, things began to escalate at home between Mom and Dad, culminating into the events of September.

I remember seeing Mom covering a bruised eye with make-up in the bathroom mirror. When she saw me watching her, she shut the door. I remember standing in the kitchen in complete confusion as Dad wrapped Mom's wrists and forearms with towels that were getting soaked with bright red blood quicker than he could wrap them. Later, I understood that she had cut her wrists.

The little me of back then, a child who needed to be held and reassured that things were going to be OK when there were blood and bruises, crying and yelling, pain and confusion all around, had to choose, albeit subconsciously, to conform to becoming a quieter, more obedient version of herself. The Obedient One she became would never think to talk back to adults or express anger at any of the chaos. She would settle for finding comfort in snuggling up against the dog on the floor or cuddling her stuffed animals under the bed. "Shhhhh, no questions, no talking! Just watch and listen and learn how to stay safe," were the messages she told herself.

But that didn't stop little me from longing for childhood fun or exploration or connection. One weekend, I was so excited when Dad told me we were taking a special fun trip, just the two of us. As he drove, I am sure I talked his ear off in anticipation of the adventure we would have. But when we got there, it turned into him leaving me alone in a strange woman's living room for hours on end while he was off having his adult kind of fun.

I envied my sister who I imagined was back home having quality time with Mom. Meanwhile, I passed the time playing my favorite Stevie Wonder album over and over in that dark, lonely living room until his music and lyrics of love washed over me enough to mask the deep pain and confusion of being lied to and alone again. I never told Mom where Dad took me. I made sure to stay obediently quiet and never let on how heartbroken I really was.

So, technically, even before that seventh year, I was already gradually concealing my true self and contorting my little one into whatever shape was required to keep the peace. But the identities that would predominantly replace my authentic little girl formally began that night in September. I can tell you with confidence that, after that night, was when I first fully bought into becoming these new identities: The Responsible One or the Obedient One, aka the Good Quiet Daughter.

*On a deeper level, after that night Mom died, I bought into the belief that I wasn't worthy of being taken care of, cherished, or nurtured.*

And how else was my little one supposed to make sense of being abandoned by her mother, who had given up on life itself? If my initial theory was correct, and Dad was really so bad that Mom needed to hurt him by doing this, what other explanation could there be for leaving us with him? I could only come up with one explanation: We weren't worth it. I wasn't even worth a mother's love.

The logic may not make sense to an adult, but that's as far as I could build the explanation with my seven-year-old mind.

There also would be no asking Dad; I knew he wouldn't be volunteering any information to help clear up the confusion. The only other thing that was clear was that quiet obedience and doing whatever was necessary to make sure my sister and I stayed in his (and His) good graces was our ticket to survival in this place that we (sometimes reluctantly) called home.

The world had now become a scary place where death and emptiness were very real. Ironically, though, after Mom left, our home actually turned out to be a lot less scary because I was able to learn the house rules well enough to keep the peace and to continue being provided for by Dad. These house rules were straightforward, black and white with few gray areas.

*For most families, the unspoken rules let a child
know: "You will be considered a good kid and I
will give you love, but only under these conditions."*

Dad's house rules, as I understood them, were to:

- Obey God.
- Follow my rules and don't question them.
- Clean my house and cook for me.
- Take responsibility for your younger sister. (You will be punished for her poor choices if you don't set a proper example and steer her correctly.)
- Do as I say, not as I do.
- Not talk too much, never talk back, stay quiet (even if I'm drunk and you're scared of me, or if I'm verbally abusive to girlfriends or unkind to pets, or if I embarrass you at your sporting events by yelling louder than everyone else because your level of play is embarrassing to me).
- Make me look good by excelling in sports. (You have my professional-athlete genes in you. I excelled at track and field and football and basketball. If you were my son, you would certainly do the same. Since you're my daughter, you can still at least get to college this way.)
- Get straight-As.
- Not become a young woman physically in front of me. (Be sure never to wear makeup or revealing clothes—baggy and boyish clothing is best.)

- Become what I approve of. (I know you love music and to sing, but the music industry is corrupt. You should be a doctor because it's honorable and will make me proud. What do you want to work with animals for, anyhow?)

- Not have children of your own, at least not if I have a say. (These are tough times, probably the "end times," and take it from me, it's too rough out there to raise children. And, of course, there is also the fact that having children of your own would get in the way of your taking care of me.)

Dad's house rules for my sister were slightly different when it came to grades and responsibilities. My understanding is that because she was younger and cried so much when Mom left he thought she was more fragile than me.

Dad obviously didn't have these written out. Some were repeatedly said to us. Some were implied or interpreted from his actions by the little me. But, as a whole, when my sister and I followed the house rules, things went relatively smoothly and we were able to have some fun along the way.

Nonetheless, our initial abandonment by Mom led me to prioritize the matter of perfecting the house rules.

*My underlying motive was to do whatever was necessary to avoid a similar abandonment by Dad.*

As I grew older, following the house rules required more and more adaptation and contortion and abandoning of myself through the subconscious assimilation of new identities. The predominant subconscious identities for my little one would ultimately become:

- The Obedient One (aka the Good Quiet Daughter).
- The Workhorse (aka the Student-Athlete).
- The Smart One (first as the Class President and later as the Doctor).
- The Doctor (essentially a merger of the Workhorse and the Smart One, who were taking orders from the Responsible One).
- The Responsible One (who believed she was responsible for both her sister and her father, and later in life for so, so many more people, except herself).

Looking back, I was quite the chameleon. But, as assuming these identities was unconscious behavior, I was not aware and had no idea. I unknowingly would fully surrender to each identity and believe that it was me. And they worked for me. They reliably kept me in Dad's good graces. I was organized, smart, and well liked. At home, I was the housekeeper. By my early teens, I could prepare an entire Thanksgiving dinner by myself. I was known to prepare tastier meals than even some of my friends' moms.

To me, it seemed like I was raising both my dad and my sister, and I would pat myself on the back for this accomplishment. This parentified child wore her accomplishments like badges of honor!

The flip side of being this little woman of the house was that I really thought I was smarter than most adults and had little respect for adult women. I saw Dad's many girlfriends, who kept coming back for more, like they were spinning in a revolving door, as ridiculous and manipulative and without anything to offer my sister and me. I'm sure they felt my lack of respect. I just saw them as weak, because every time Dad showed very obvious signs of disrespect, they forgave him. I just shook my head, thinking, *They blame him yet think they can change him. How can it be that a child can see more than an adult?* So I grew up convinced I would do everything in my power to never give anyone reason to disrespect me. It wouldn't be until many years in the future that I would learn that someone else's actions are not a reflection of me at all. None of us actually have control of or responsibility for someone else's thoughts, words, or deeds. In hindsight, how interesting it is that, as I witnessed the women come and go from our life and the blatant disrespect, my coping mechanism became to also disrespect women, especially myself.

And since I had mastered the rules of Dad's house, and since his house could get super scary, I believed, of course, that I was fully prepared to apply these same rules to the real and scary world. *Bring on "adulting"; it should be a piece of cake!*

Hah! Boy, did I have a rude awakening coming.

The consequence of only being focused on following rules was that I had no idea what I really liked or wanted for myself. For example, one of Dad's girlfriends put it in his head that since I was so smart I should go to a private boarding school instead of the local public high school. I then was required to interview at two boarding schools. The whole time, I was scared to death of leaving home and being separated from what was familiar to me, but I never spoke up. I went through the motions of the interviews, following orders. Eventually, Dad called it off. I suspect he also didn't want me to leave home. I was relieved.

The next time, someone else convinced him I should go to one of our country's finest military academies. He then instructed me to choose between applying to either the Naval Academy or West Point. I chose to apply to West Point because it was closest to home. I went through all of the multiple rounds required for the application, including the physical aptitude exam and getting an official nomination by a US senator. Ultimately, I was accepted. Yet, the entire time, I was merely going through the motions because it was what I needed to do to be obedient and get Dad's approval. I never once thought about the other applicants, who were genuinely passionate about serving our country and for whom it would have meant the world to get in.

*I never thought of doing anything else*
*because my decisions were not coming from*
*the place of knowing what I really wanted*
*to do or what I felt passionate about.*

Luckily for our country, I finally snapped out of my trance of obedience when I read the acceptance letter signed by the president of the United States. There was a piece of that letter that said something along these lines: "Don't do this because your coaches, your teachers, or your parents want you to do it.

Do this because you're proud to serve your country and want this for yourself." Something inside me finally said, *You can't do this.* Then, for the first time in years, I spoke up, despite risking the loss of approval from Dad. I wish I could tell you I learned to listen to that voice more often, but I did not.

*Blind unquestioning, going through the motions, making choices from a place of seeking approval, and avoiding abandonment had become my MO.*

At first, I could usually assert myself with friends when it came to what felt good to me, even if I never could to Dad. During the summer, when we still lived in the house where Mom lived, while Dad was off at work, one of my older friends from around the neighborhood would come by the house to smoke weed that we found hidden in one of Dad's drawers. On most occasions, I smoked it with her, but eventually I realized I really didn't like lying to Dad. I finally spoke up and told her I wasn't interested in smoking anymore. She tried to make a logical case that marijuana was a plant and therefore nothing to be ashamed of, but that case didn't hold up to the fact that I wasn't even ten years old yet or that without me she'd need to get her own supply.

At first, I was happy to have stood up for what felt right to me, but then it seemed to me that each time I stood my ground I lost friends. With the exception of inside the school walls, where kids were obligated to interact with other students or teachers, I wound up spending more and more time alone.

After saying no to smoking weed, I usually stayed inside to read while my sister played outside with that same older girl and the others in her group in which I was no longer welcome. Then, one day, the doorbell rang. To my surprise, I opened the door to a group of smiling girls. "We want you to play with us again. Let's shake on it," they said. I reached out my hand to shake and one of them smashed an overripe banana into my palm. As banana flesh oozed between my fingers, my heart sank. The girls ran away, along with my sister, laughing.

I closed the door and went back to being alone. Everything about that house where Mom once lived and that neighborhood stunk like pain and loneliness to me.

I was relieved when Dad was finally able to move us out of that lower-income small town to a more ethnically diverse middle-class city suburb. It was my chance to put the memories of the place we had previously called home behind me and try to fit in with new friends. Initially, it seemed much easier there to fit in. I was drawn to what I knew and immediately gelled with a few kids who also, coincidentally, enjoyed smoking weed after school. But as I met more people in my honors classes, on the track field, and on the basketball court, passing time smoking no longer made sense to me. I naturally saw less and less of that group.

My closest friends were kids who lived on the same circular street as us. Our "Circle-hood" was a neighborhood of townhouses with a large shared backyard in the middle of them. We all walked to school together, and the summers felt much less lonely. Through the sports team I joined, I was also able to find a few more friends, but many of them lived in big houses in prettier neighborhoods. Since we spent so many hours together, either in the classroom or competing at sports, I managed to build some connections with them even though their worlds seemed very different from mine.

I'm not sure how the other kids spent their evenings, but once school was out and my sports practice ended, I would head home to do homework, clean the house, and go promptly to bed. Meanwhile, Dad was either out doing "adult things" until the early morning or in his bedroom watching TV. My sister was there, and in hindsight, I do wish I had spent more time with her, but she was much more social than I ever was. She spent most of her free time playing with her friends as opposed to staying inside to do chores or homework with me. Eventually, she didn't want much to do with me at all, as I was still trying to play the role of her mother. Just as any daughter needs to separate from her mom, as a teenager, she wanted no part of me. Slowly, my at-home reality became lonely again.

Then, one weekend, one of the girls in my science class who was also on the varsity basketball and track teams with me invited me to sleep over at her big, pretty house on the hill. I was so excited to get a glimpse of what her home life might be like. Maybe they would have the dream family life, filled with curiosity and caring, where they were always enjoying each other's company. I imagined they'd eat dinner together as a family and spend hours just talking and laughing while playing board games.

Once I was finally there, I can't recall how we actually passed the time, but I do recall her parents expressing genuine interest in their children's lives, and I didn't notice any specific house rules or conditions they had to follow.

My friend set up a sleeping area for us in the basement, with a sleeping bag for each of us, and we watched late-night TV before going to sleep. We had just turned off the TV and had fallen to sleep when her older brother came home from his night out and walked down the steps into the basement. He was a really tall, skinny senior in our high school. I actually only knew who he was because I had a bit of a crush on one of his friends. His friend was one of those guys who looked like a movie star, down to the sexy stubble of a goatee, and much too mature looking really to be in high school. But, in my mind, my friend's brother was just that hot senior's sidekick. I remember in school I might say the obligatory hello to my friend's brother while trying to get the attention of my crush.

I think her brother's bedroom actually may have been located down there in the back end of the basement, so I assumed that was why he was coming down the stairs. But instead of turning toward the door at the back of the basement, he surprisingly walked quietly over to our sleeping area and tugged on my sleeping bag to wake me. He hadn't realized the noise of his coming home late at night had already woken me. With his sister lying right there next to me, he whispered, "Hey, come back to my room with me," while simultaneously grabbing at my forearm to come with.

"No," I answered firmly, but still in a whisper, while trying to pull my arm back to my side. This happened several times before he changed his approach and sat down next to me on the floor. With him this close, I was now unable to free my arm from his grip.

All at once, I was completely confused, absolutely annoyed, and angered enough to want to scream if it weren't for his sister who was still (I assumed) sleeping on the floor right next to us. So, I didn't scream. I remained frozen and quiet. I said nothing as he directed my fingers over his thickened penis and used my hand to rub one out.

My voice was gone. I held my breath. I felt ashamed. I was disgusted that he would do this in front of his sister. Was she awake? Would she blame me for this and think that I was the disgusting one? Would I lose another friend for standing my ground? I gave up and let it happen. And then he left. Another night of silence while too confused to process the events.

Oh wait! I knew what to do. Be the Obedient One. Stay quiet, go back to bed.

*Over and over, I continued to abandon myself*
*as I took on more of these identities.*

At first, Lou was still with me enough to keep me pursuing my many interests. For instance, I loved animals, especially dogs. We always had at least one dog in our home, and I formed close bonds with each one. I loved to think of myself as a sort of dog whisperer.

I also loved all things musical, especially singing and dancing to music. I found I could pursue my love of singing and dancing through attending a summer music camp or joining our Sunday school chorus. But I quickly learned the hard way that there was actually a big difference between the "approved" and "unapproved" ways of following this particular interest of mine. Apparently, the unapproved way was my showing off my midriff onstage while having a small part in our summer music camp's performance of *Joseph and the Technicolor Dreamcoat*. This unapproved participation in singing and dancing called for me being beaten across my backside, legs, and lower back with a metal curtain rod. Not only did the play's title sound too blasphemous, but in Dad's opinion I also had apparently led my sister astray, because she was only following in her big sister's footsteps by wanting to be in the musical, too.

The approved ways of being involved in music, on the other hand, would turn out to be singing in the youth choir at church, playing flute and piccolo in the high school marching band, or singing a duet with a friend in a high school talent show.

I somehow was able to squeeze dancing in for the duration of one season of gymnastics, where I learned to do a floor routine with less tumbling and more of the dance elements. My routine was choreographed to the song "If I Were a Rich Man" from *Fiddler on the Roof*, and this was one of the few and only times in my athletic career that I can remember thoroughly enjoying a sporting competition. I was thrilled when the opposing team's coach approached me at the end of the competition and said I should become a dancer. Of course, I knew that would never fly with Dad and his house rules, but it gave me secret validation that in another life that is probably what I would have been. A professional dancer.

As for my interest in drawing, I used to steal time any chance I could get to draw animals, especially my dogs, and even portraits of my sister. In elementary school, I recall being so proud that my teacher posted my drawing of the Taj Mahal in the center of the class bulletin board, and it was even clear to me that my version looked a lot like the actual photo we were asked to replicate.

By middle school, my drawings allowed me to be part of a group that was able to spend the day painting a mural on the art classroom's walls. On my assigned area, I drew and painted a ceiling-to-floor rendering of E.T., the extraterrestrial, from the movie. But by high school, as I was becoming those other identities, the Obedient One, the Smart One, and The Student-Athlete, I stopped drawing altogether. I don't think I even tried to find an illustration class as an elective.

Back at the house where Mom had lived, I enjoyed reading books of fantasy and magic, witches and wizards, but since (you've probably guessed it) those were more unapproved interests, I had to choose to put them aside. Fortunately for me, by high school Dad figured that if I was reading I must be getting ahead and prepping for school, so he stopped inquiring about the content of my reading. Thankfully, I got away with sneaking some fantasy novels and other unapproved reading materials in here and there.

As I remember it, by the time I was in high school, Dad had stopped asking me about much of anything that I was up to or interested in at all. So, on the rare occasion that he did, I would seize the opportunity and try to tell him every detail of my day, squeezing in as many words as possible while he was still willing to entertain me. But then I would quickly lose his ear and have to get back to the chores and the responsibilities waiting for me.

*I deeply craved even the tiniest moments of attention from someone who loved me, and this reinforced me in doing whatever I needed to get more of them.*

Meanwhile, all opportunities to pursue my childhood interests were vanishing. As you know, I didn't end up going to West Point, but I did choose to attend our state university, where I received both an academic scholarship and an athletic scholarship. The scholarship rules were that I would lose the academic scholarship if I didn't maintain a certain grade-point average; by having an athletic scholarship in track and field, my bases were covered.

Since I had already won Dad's approval and fully adopted the identity of the Workhorse on the path to becoming the Doctor, I thought maybe at the university I could possibly still hold on to my love of music. I still vividly recall the day when we were asked to sign up for our college classes and I beelined straight over to the marching band's table.

"Wait, you can't do that," the registrars explained. "This is Division One NCAA, Big East Sports now. Your time will be dedicated to training and competing in track and field at least three-plus hours a day, and on most weekends and some holidays. Those are the same hours that the marching band holds its practice and plays for the football games. You'll have to choose."

The inner dialogue that followed went something like this. *Hmmm. If I gave up the athletic scholarship, what would that mean? It means Dad would flip out on me. Am I really smart enough anyway to keep that GPA without the athletic scholarship as backup? Nope. I'd probably just end up losing the scholarship and dropping out of school for not being able to pay the tuition. Besides, everyone knows it's rare to have a lucrative career in music or dance. It's probably best I stick to becoming a doctor like I'm supposed to.*

And at that moment, just like that, I gave up on my interest in music and dance.

*Meanwhile, somewhere in a dark corner inside me, Lou curled up and cried from the pain of abandonment again.*

*Little by little, one small choice followed by another, everything that Lou was happy doing disappeared.*

In the midst of my efforts to win approval and avoid abandonment from Dad, I was abandoning Lou (myself) over and over again, although I did make weak attempts here and there to bring a little joy into Lou's life. For instance, at the university, I tried to appreciate even the smallest times I was outside in nature or near animals. Since the university had a strong agricultural department, there were miles of farmland to explore. While my university track team ran alongside the farms and farm animals, I would at least pretend I was part of an exploration as I used to do often as a child in the woods by our house. Yeah, I know. I said it was a weak attempt.

The saddest part was that each time I tried to squeeze my foot into the glass slipper of those identities (the Obedient One, the Workhorse/Student-Athlete, or the insidiously developing Responsible One), the more I convinced myself that those shoes fit. My identification with each role was being reinforced the longer I played out the different parts. I had subconsciously created these personas to protect me and help me just get by in a scary world, but somewhere along the way, I began believing they were the real me.

*I was going through the necessary motions to earn praise, attention, and approval, get scholarships, and have my basic needs met, but it was always at the cost of turning my back on Lou and my authenticity.*

So, that's the summary of how easy it was to abandon myself, even when you'd think that would be the last thing I'd want to do after having already been hugely abandoned by Mom. But by fully buying in and becoming these identities, that's exactly what I did. I headed straight down the rabbit hole of trying to become something I wasn't and losing years of my life in the process.

Why would I or anyone do this to herself? I now know that it was because deep inside I thought I wasn't good enough just being me as I was. But thankfully, at the bottom of that rabbit hole was the truth that I was actually running away from this painful belief about myself.

*I'm sure it is no surprise to you that in my efforts to run away from what I didn't want, I coincidentally ran right smack into exactly that.*

Life allowed me the opportunity to finally feel what I was trying to avoid feeling on that fateful night in September when I was seven.

In the following sections, I'll introduce you to each of my false identities and how each was created to protect, assist, or help me (Lou) in some way.

*Why else would anyone agree to ignore their dreams and forgo their needs, and lose so many years of her life, if there wasn't some form of secondary gain to her in so doing?*

CHAPTER 3

# *The Obedient One (aka the Good Daughter)*

As mentioned earlier, right after Mom died, it made perfect sense to little me (Lou) that obedience was the ticket to stay in the good graces of Dad and God. As the Obedient One, Lou made sure to do all that was necessary to be in His good graces. Lou invited Jesus into her heart as her savior. She signed up to be baptized in their Baptist church. Lou memorized and followed the lyrics to Sunday School songs such as these with devotion.

(Sung acapella)

"O-B-E-D-IENCE, obedience is the very best way to show that you believe."

Or, "Trust and obey, for there's no other way, to be happy... than to trust and obey."

*Unfortunately, somehow Lou selectively forgot*
*other songs with more inspiring vibes to which*
*she could have just as easily chosen to cling.*

Lou could have sung:

"This little light of mine, I'm gonna let it shine…"

Or, "I've got joy, joy, joy down in my heart…"

Lou also thought it was her duty to study the Bible with the same dedication that she would study her schoolbooks. She sang in the youth choir fervently and attended Vacation Bible School (VBS, if you were one of the cool kids) in the summer. Without exaggeration, almost every week, she went to Sunday school, sometimes attending both morning and evening services. One summer, Lou got it in her head that she wanted to teach the other children on our "Circle-hood." She set up her own summer Bible study class, complete with an easel, singing, and snacks for the kids.

Depending on whether it was Dad who took us to church or the church bus that picked up us "underprivileged kids," we were indoctrinated into many kinds of Christian denominations including Fundamental Baptist, Roman Catholic, and even Interdenominational. Dad was covering all the bases for his girls. But Dad preferred the do-as-I-say, not-as-I-do approach to parenting, so usually we were sent on the church bus to attend services without Dad. And, no matter the religion, obedience seemed to be a common theme. Lou still enjoyed most of it as she believed it would bring her closer to the God who loves all of us unconditionally, especially children.

God's rules and conditions, as Lou understood them, were:

- Say the "Sinner's Prayer" and invite God into your heart.
- No impure thought or action (see the Ten Commandments).
- If you found that you've broken either of the above rules, as long as you had what was often termed "fire insurance" (for escaping hellfire), you may simply confess, asked for forgiveness, and then get back on the straight and narrow.
- Be a virgin until marriage.
- Love and forgive everyone (in other words, turn the other cheek).

Of course, eventually Lou noticed that not everyone in the church was following these rules, and so, as inquisitive children do, she started asking questions.

*Why do the many different churches all think THEIR rules are THE rules?*

*If God loves everyone unconditionally, then why are there rules and conditions to deserve His grace?*

*If there's a Him and His Son/Child, then doesn't it make the most sense that the Holy Spirit is a Her?*

In spite of these developing questions, Lou remained the consummate rule follower. She was also fascinated by the idea that there was a being capable of creating the rules of nature and the rules of the universe. Just pondering the sheer magnitude of that filled her with awe and wonder. She reminded herself that in the much bigger picture of our Universe there were stars and planets and so many things bigger than the tiny events in her little life.

*In this vast universe, she could be hopeful that the Bible verse that read "All things [in the Universe] work together for good" (Romans 8:28) was true.*

Lou repeated this verse from Romans like a mantra to herself whenever she found her mind drifting toward more painful questions like, *Why did I have to be born into a home with so much emotional volatility, chaos, and sadness?*

Lou had hoped in her heart that maybe one day she'd get to see that good actually could come of what made very little sense to her. Maybe one day she'd be given the answers to her ever-growing list of questions like:

*What in life was so horrible that Mom spent so much time crying and Dad spend so much time yelling?*

*Why didn't Mom stop to think of the potential impact it would have on a seven-year-old to witness her slashed wrists with blood everywhere, while Dad tried to cover them with bandages and help hide the scene from our view? Even Hollywood moviemakers knew not to allow children to view horror scenes.*

*Why, if Dad was really such a villain, would Mom turn her back on us and leave her own children with this man?*

*Were we so unworthy that she'd use her own children as weapons to punish Dad by saying, "Here, you deal with them, I'm out!"*

Yet, from a still more hopeful place deep inside of her, a place that was capable of believing one day she'd see things "work together for good," the magical idea that she could receive direction from the mysterious "still, small voice" that the pastor of her church always spoke of somehow made perfect sense to Lou. I'm not sure whether it was due to all of the Bible studies or to reading all of the magical fantasy books Lou so loved to read, but the idea of hearing a voice speaking to her that no one else could hear did seem normal.

Lou would hear that voice on random occasions, and although it was very difficult to tell whether it was coming from inside or outside her head, the voice was always clear and definitive. Like when one afternoon in high school, while sitting in the school's auditorium waiting for them to announce the winner to a raffle, Lou felt an odd sense of knowing and said to herself, *They're going to pick me, aren't they?*

Then the voice answered, "Yes."

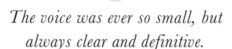

*The voice was ever so small, but
always clear and definitive.*

Sure enough, within minutes, they called Lou's name (well, they said *Lana*) to come down and pick up the gift she'd won.

Or like that other time, during Sunday school when Lou was tired and preferred just to daydream instead of listening to the teacher. That odd, indescribable knowing sensation arrived, and the voice said to Lou, "Pay attention." This time Lou must have been feeling feisty and talked back to it by replying, *Why should I? I'm too tired.*

The small, clear, direct voice answered, "Because he'll ask you to tell him what you learned when you get home."

*Hmmm, that's odd. Dad never asks about Sunday school,* Lou thought to herself, but she went ahead and paid attention anyway.

And sure enough, unlike any other Sunday, Dad wanted to talk when she got home. He eventually asked, "What did they teach you today in Sunday school?"

Lou was so shocked and amazed that she jumped to explain to Dad the details of what had happened and how there was a voice that told her to pay attention because he'd ask. Dad just smiled as if for him it reinforced that the Obedient One was still in His good graces.

In time, however, Lou didn't hear that voice anymore—or, more accurately, I didn't listen to that voice again for many years.

# CHAPTER 4

# The Workhorse (aka the Student-Athlete)

"Give me ten," he'd say to us before bed. One could assume ten push-ups at ten years old shouldn't be too difficult, right? Someone that small had very little weight to push off the ground anyway, right?

Well, that was indeed true for Lou. She'd drop down, making sure to keep her skinny body perfectly parallel to the ground in proper technique, chin just touching the floor, and then push herself back up...eight, nine, ten! At the ten count, she'd pop up off the floor, chest out from being proud to receive Dad's approval and relieved to know she was still in his good graces. She was then allowed to head to bed without a snag.

Our younger sister wouldn't be so lucky. She'd try hard but could never seem to get past the first couple of push-ups before she'd start shaking and drop to the floor with her arms collapsing under her. Dad appeared determined to prove to her she could do this like her sister could and so she was instructed to try again. "You both carry my [strong professional athlete] genes," he'd remind us for what seemed like the hundredth time. Again and again, her arms shook and her skinny little body would collapse in fatigue.

Dad eventually considered an alternative route and proclaimed, "Fine! Just at least hold yourself up for the count of ten." With her arms still trembling, and with Lou holding her breath, no longer feeling as proud of her accomplishments as she watched her sister fall further out of Dad's good graces, our sister finally made it to the full count of ten. Together, we then were excused to bed.

On subsequent nights, Dad allowed my sister to do the "girl version" of push-ups (clearly implying it was a "less-than" version of a push-up). She could do them with knees remaining on the ground and only needing to push up the weight of her upper body. As long as our sister did this version and I did the (implied better) "boy version," we could do our push-ups in sync and all would be well.

Lou was well on her way toward proving she could also serve to be a great substitute for the son Dad never had.

And just as Dad predicted, Lou became a star track and field athlete, specializing, as he did, in hurdles and sprints. He taught Lou the proper hurdle form, with arm motions that easily allowed the knee to pass under while quickly planting her leg after the hurdle was cleared. Lou could see that passing along his knowledge of sports really made Dad light up and, very likely, had he been blessed with a son (or a child to teach with an equal passion for sports), that son/child would've become a professional athlete as well with his help.

As for Lou, she was just satisfied knowing that if Dad was happy that meant there would be peace, so she continued to soak up his training.

Let me be clear. Dad was absolutely Lou's hero. In shop class she carved a wood plaque that read, "The Best Dad in the World." But just as much as she loved him, she desperately wanted his approval. If all Lou had to do to please him was continue doing the preferred "boy version" of push-ups, hiding her female body under baggy clothes, and wearing no makeup, then so be it.

Speaking of being more like Dad's son, there was one rainy Saturday afternoon when track practice had to be held inside of the school library. On inclement weather days, our practice was limited to stationary drills and perfecting techniques. Our coach set up makeshift hurdles with paper tape that we'd need to jump over. This one specific afternoon, an onlooking child watched with his mom as Lou leaped over the paper tape and Coach critiqued my form.

Lou could hear the child ask, "Mom, is that a boy or a girl?" She couldn't hear the mom's answer as they walked away, but the question stopped Lou in her tracks, and she burst into tears.

"They can't even tell I'm a girl," Lou said through watering eyes as she looked up at the coach. Lou could feel that pain that I had been trying to push down, the pain of believing that Dad wanted a son. Why else would Lou be made to go through all of this sports routine? It hadn't occurred to me that Dad was just teaching me to do the only thing he knew how to do really well, thinking that was how he could contribute to our future.

It was even more confusing to get treated like a son because it seemed to suit Dad just fine that we were girls when he explained that our Christian duty as daughters was to also do all of the house chores and cook the majority of the meals.

But even as I was beginning to convince myself that becoming a substitute son was what would keep Dad around, Lou still longed to do the things she saw (and imagined) that the other girls her age were doing. She often daydreamed about questions like:

*What would it feel like to put on makeup and paint my face like beautiful art on a canvas, or to choose colorful form-fitting outfits to wear?*

*What would it feel like to be relaxed and soft instead of tough and brave and on guard?*

*What if it was OK to ask for help or to have someone rush over to pick up that heavy item for me?*

Lou could admit she was tired of needing to be so strong all the time or of it being a requirement always to have to do so much for herself without parental support. She could feel the void of nurturing feminine energy in our home.

*There was certainly plenty of competitive, aggressive, and productive (masculine) energy in our home, but very little energy that was associated with peace, stillness, and creative (feminine) flow.*

In the name of excelling, Dad was committed to giving me and my sister a competitive edge. "No one remembers second place," he would often say. On random evenings after he got off work and on sporadic weekends throughout the summer, Dad would pack us into the car and drive us to a special athletic training ground that we called the Hill. We hated the Hill. "Please don't let it be the Hill today," we'd say under our breaths. From our point of view, the Hill was way too steep for two tiny preteen girls to be required to conquer. And the view was ominous from the bottom. The Hill itself was actually just a side street in a residential area across town, and certainly can't be compared to the kind of street hills I've seen as an adult while living in San Francisco. Thank goodness we did not grow up there!

We were convinced that Dad drove around for hours in search of a hill like this one as a means to torture us while training our legs into their inevitable pro athlete shape. He would drop us off at the bottom, then drive to the top, and stand in the middle of the street peering down at us, usually still in his work suit and dress shoes. At his signal, we were to run up the entire steep hill to meet him.

For Lou, this exercise felt like a punishment. The foreseeable reward for succeeding was to be greeted by him at the top with further instructions on how to run back down and come up again. On occasion, he'd mix it up and have us try to run up the second half of it facing backward. Each time, upon reaching the last stretch where the Hill had its most vertical incline, our thighs and calves would burn in pain and stiffen up to the point that we literally looked like we were moving in slow motion. And that's how it felt as well.

It was hard to see the point of this kind of exercise. To Lou, it was pure torture. But I was developing the understanding that working hard was how one gets ahead in life, that this was what was required to excel. I also believed this was what was required to keep the peace in our home, to remain in good graces, and to get our basic needs met, so I instructed Lou to stop complaining, keep quiet, and just run the damned hill. As much as Lou hated running the Hill, I made sure there would be no back talk to Dad. There would be no speaking up and asking if we could please skip the Hill today. There would only be the Obedient One and the developing Workhorse, even if it meant bottling up my emotions underneath those personas.

Sure enough, the training on the Hill did help us earn our keep on the track, like a prized racehorse in the making. We (Lou and I) set and broke multiple school records in the hurdles, sprints, and relays. On the outside, I always held it together; but on the inside, before every race, Lou would feel extreme nausea and panic. So, I proceeded to shove Lou's emotions even further down since she didn't realize we were usually the favorite to win and there could be no looking weak in front of Dad or the competition.

Every time we crouched in the starting position waiting for that gun to go off, it felt like an eternity for Lou. Most times Lou was almost to the point of tears and begging to be freed from the misery of another race. She often thought of those horses working on the city streets pulling tourists in a carriage behind them in the sweltering summer heat. Pulling a carriage looked easy for the horse to the onlooker, but she imagined they were just as miserable as she was.

In the hot sun and in our respective lanes, with our spiked shoe-covered feet behind us propped in the starting blocks, leaning forward over our arms with our fingers balancing our weight on the rubber track surface, we waited. Then the starting gun would explode as the signal to propel us forward into the race. Once we came off of the starting blocks, Lou learned to blank out the noise of the crowd and the thoughts in her head and just run. As I directed my focus on keeping proper sprint form, Lou tried to make the race more fun by keeping her eyes locked onto the back of the runner ahead and pretending we were reeling her in as we got closer, one at a time. My favorite part of the race was always the last corner, the turn just before the straightaway leading to the finish line. By then I would've caught and passed enough of the runners either to win or to medal in the top three, and I had certainty that either option would keep Lou in Dad's good graces.

From that last turn until the end of the race, I'd run as hard and fast as I could, digging from deep within me, because, for both Lou and me, the finish line meant it was over, if only for a moment. No matter how much pain Lou was in, no matter how much our leg muscles would lock up, and yes, probably thanks to having run that dreaded Hill, I would make sure to end it really strong, running straight through the finish line. I never slowed down until I was well across the line.

I suspect that Dad and my coaches thought my display of full-out strength and determination at the end of every race meant I really wanted to win, or even possibly, that I hated to lose, but what it really demonstrated was how badly I knew Lou wanted it to be over.

In summary, the truth behind my inner struggle during races is as follows.

- **First third of the race:** Lou would never allow me to be the one to "explode right out of the gate," as much as Dad and my coaches wished I would. I was a slow starter simply because I was still having a figurative internal argument with Lou, who just really didn't want to be there.

- **Second third of the race:** Intense focus and only give attention to form, breath, and what was in right front of me.

- **Last third of the race:** Run like hell so Lou could just be done with it already and I could gain the approval I believed was needed to survive.

*Intense focus and only giving attention to form, breath, and what was right in front of me proved to be a skill Lou taught me that I could use to my advantage in the future.*

And, despite the inner struggle, it still worked for me. I won A LOT of races. I collected multiple trophies and medals, and my effort successfully paid for my undergraduate education at an NCAA Division I university. In hindsight, had I ever actually "exploded out of the gate" and really tested what my body was made of, I have no doubt I would have proved Dad correct by becoming an elite athlete. But even the thought of doing more races without a clear end in sight, without a clear finish line, made Lou want to crawl under a rock.

Subconsciously, I rationalized with her that we needed to keep doing this just enough to pay our dues to Dad for not abandoning us. I was determined to pay my dues and earn his favor, even if it meant I continued to ignore and bottle up Lou's building anger and resistance under the surface, keeping it from breaking free.

What Lou was also noticing, which I wasn't aware of yet, was that it was very lonely to be the Workhorse. I didn't develop any real friendships in college outside of the circle of teammates I ran with day in and day out and during weekend track meet bus trips. They were amazingly talented and fun young women, who all seemed to love our sport. We were accomplished enough that our relay team was flown to Jamaica by the university to participate in a big relay event in Kingston. We stayed at a hotel with a big, beautiful pool that had a fountain in the middle. Since this was an international event, we weren't expected to place very well in the race, so much of the pressure of winning was removed. Without the added pressure, this was the first time I allowed Lou to fully enjoy the moment with these young women. Sometimes Lou felt bad that she hadn't gotten to know them any better.

A day in my college life was all work and very little play, and this felt familiar and normal to me, even if it was sad and lonely for

Lou. I'd get up around 6 AM, attend classes (including the premed prep classes and afternoon science lab) until approximately 3 PM. I'd squeeze in a meal on the go somewhere as I walked across campus to get to the next class. I'd then head to the athletic dome to meet the team for training and weight lifting until 6 PM. Dinner was in the dining hall somewhere around 6:30 or 7:00 PM. It was then back to the dorm for homework, studies, sleep, wake up, repeat.

I found some comfort in literally clinging to my high school boyfriend, who was on the same campus, as a refuge from the daily grind. He, too, was a top performer for one of our university's sports teams and he spent as many hours in training and on weekend road trips as I did. On occasion, when he was on the road, the track girls could convince me to go to a party on campus with them. But for the most part, I was in my usual routine of following the rules, being the Obedient One and the Student-Athlete, with my ultimate sights set on graduating, getting married, and never having to beat my body into submission in the name of athletic competition again.

As you could probably guess, I had incorrectly calculated that graduation and marriage to a high school sweetheart would bring me freedom and closer to paying off the debt I owed to Dad for not abandoning me as Mom had. Even in college, I still believed my value was in how well I could follow Dad's rules. I maintained my commitment to gaining his approval with triumphs on the track.

At this point, I was preparing also to assume a new persona, the Doctor, who would surely seal the deal. This was how I could be confident that Dad would always approve of me.

I believed my value to the university was clearly to make the coaches proud by winning as many races as I could. Meanwhile, I somehow would still keep up enough of my grades to get into medical school. I know now that Lou could have easily told me at what cost this success would be earned, but at the time I was still ignoring her in exchange for doing what the Workhorse and Obedient One thought was in her best interest.

*Seeing my value only as it related to other people's expectations of me had become my way of life, but I couldn't yet see at what cost.*

It would have been a smoother road if I had just noticed Lou's diamonds and pearls of wisdom right away. But I seemed to prefer to learn the hard way.

*Life has a way of getting our attention when we are ignoring our own inner voice of wisdom.*

For me, that nudge came in the form of a preventable medical illness.

At the beginning of the track season, we were introduced to our team trainer whose duty was whipping us into top shape. We would run as a large group across the campus as we worked our way up to six-mile runs. For most of us sprinters, since we weren't built for the cross-country team, six miles was a really long haul. We'd end our workouts in the gym lifting weights, doing isometrics, and finally stretching, before calling it a day. We were praised when we pushed ourselves to the point where many of us needed to bend over on the side of the road (or track) to vomit, wipe our mouths, and keep going.

Most nights after track practice I'd lie in bed with my arms and legs stretched out, their muscles too painful to move. On occasion, I could feel Lou wondering if I had lost my mind to volunteer for so much pain, but I rationalized that it was a normal part of training. Eventually I learned to go numb. I'd detach myself from what Lou was feeling and rationally and logically remind myself that this pain was just a by-product from the lactic acid breaking down the muscle fibers that we were purposefully remodeling to be "better, stronger, faster," like the narrator on *The Six Million Dollar Man* would explain.

Then one afternoon, on our usual route, I couldn't keep up with the group for more than a half of a mile and quickly fell to the back of the pack. I was embarrassed and confused as the star athlete who should have been leading the pack. This went on for at least a week, until the team trainer finally scheduled a meeting with our head coach after practice. The team trainer said things very similar to what Dad would say when he would yell at me from the bleachers whenever I wasn't performing to his satisfaction. The trainer told the head coach something along the lines of "She's not even trying. She has our scholarship money and she's wasting it!"

Thankfully, the head coach gave me the benefit of the doubt, and instead of making assumptions, she got curious.

She asked me questions such as: "What exactly happens when you feel too tired to keep up?"

I explained to her that it was hard to take in a full breath, that my heart would race faster than usual and my legs felt like lead weights I could no longer carry, so I had to slow down and eventually stop. Once I stopped and caught my breath, I could start running again, but by then the rest of the team was way ahead. As I told my version of the story, I saw what I perceived to be the trainer's look of disgust, and to me, his eyes spoke volumes. I imagined he was thinking, *She's a quitter and she doesn't have what it takes.*

I think it may have been obvious to everyone else that I didn't have the same drive to beat the competition at all costs that my teammates did (I was called "cupcake" because I'd smile at people on the starting line instead of "mean muggin," like everyone else). But a quitter was one thing I was not. So I don't believe the trainer actually said I was a quitter, but that's what I imagined his attitude about me was as he stood there with his arms folded and shaking his head.

The head coach did seem genuinely interested in finding out what was happening, ultimately sending me to the campus infirmary to get checked out. At the infirmary, they drew blood and asked me questions about my family's possible genetic history with sickle cell anemia or any other heart disease. I explained that Dad had a heart attack when I was thirteen years old, but we were pretty sure it was probably due to smoking and that ever since he stopped smoking he seemed fine.

My results came back that I had severe anemia. Just a point lower and they said I would have needed a blood transfusion. (If you are a science-minded reader, my hemoglobin level was 7.0 g/dl, while the normal level for an over-eighteen-year-old girl is 14.0g/dl.)

They called my condition *marching* or *foot strike impact anemia.* This is a form of mechanical hemolytic anemia that is found in many soldiers and elite athletes, especially runners. The general idea was that the full impact of my foot striking the ground in multiple consecutive training sessions of high intensity, combined with having an improper breathing technique—as I had never officially learned how to breathe for long-distance running because I had trained for sprints—sent repetitive shock waves into my feet and radiating up my lower legs, causing the red blood cells to rupture (hemolysis). Since this -lysis was happening too fast for my body to recover by producing enough new red blood cells to replace the ruptured ones before I ran again, it resulted in my blood having a lowered oxygen-carrying capacity and iron deficiency.

The doctor explained that the job of our intact red blood cells is to carry oxygen from the lungs to the rest of the body by binding the oxygen to the hemoglobin within the red cell. Without iron, your body can't make enough red blood cells, and without enough intact functioning red cells, your body is starved of oxygen. So, in my case, it was deduced, that I was not breathing in enough oxygen and that the little oxygen I was able to breathe in still could not be effectively delivered to my body where the demand for more oxygen was higher than usual during these intense workouts.

To treat the anemia and avoid needing a blood transfusion, as well as avoiding a long list of potentially serious complications, I was given iron supplements and instructed not to run with the team until my hemoglobin level was in a safer range. *Wait, what?! Hallelujah!* I could hear Lou shout. For the first time ever, we were given an officially prescribed break!

This prescribed break from the relentless punishment of my body felt so heaven sent. The break meant that: A) I was still being the Obedient One, but this time Lou would be completely happy to comply with the orders given; and B) I had actual permission to rest and do nothing, even if just for this brief glorious moment. Furthermore, C) the team trainer had to formally apologize to me for his contribution in my feeling like a useless quitter (an unexpected bonus).

Over the next four weeks, while building up my iron stores, I also had to gradually build up a tolerance for running. Week one was limited to just walking. Week two, I would alternate running and walking. Week three, I was given more running, more isometrics, and more weight lifting, but all at a gradual, steady pace.

*The exercise was tailored around how I felt while doing it.*

With this new routine, I was eventually brought to the best shape of my life. The slow, consistent, buildable approach was the complete opposite of the usual all-or-none, continuous, and unpredictable stints of maxed-out intensity.

*This new approach to training made*
*the progress feel effortless.*

With the new regimen, I didn't shy away from the workout "burn," and yet relentlessly pushing myself through the pain was no longer the focus. The intensity was only experienced in small doses, with me having full control of how far I wanted to take it based solely on how I was feeling. The old no-pain-no-gain, push-yourself-to-exhaustion model was always stressful, always of high impact; although it did produce some record-setting results, it was not sustainable. And for Lou, it was never enjoyable.

Prior to this prescribed rest, I had always been pouring energy from an empty cup, squeezing out every last drop, and leaving myself and Lou depleted and exhausted.

If you are someone who truly enjoys intense, punishing workouts, please remember that this is my story. Possibly yours could include a million ways to do that same no-pain-no-gain method better, like incorporating regular rest, using proper breathing techniques, and coming to play full-out with a refreshed mindset. But I couldn't see that at that time. That's the thing about our own stories. We have blind spots.

*I could only have the mindset/perspective/
view from where I was at that time, with
my combined lifetime of experiences and
conditioning up until that point.*

What I know now is that my body (and Lou) were thanking me for embracing this new and different approach.

*It was the first glimpse of how good it could
feel to put my own well-being and self-
care first. But yet it still required someone
outside of me, this time the head coach,
to give me permission and make it so.*

I had not yet realized that if it hadn't been for the coach, I would have collapsed and needed a blood transfusion to revive me from nothing short of complete neglect and abandonment of my own needs and warning signs. Thank you, Coach, you were like an angel to me.

My approach to life at that time could be summed up like this:

Instead of questioning, I simply assumed all of those years that all of the rules and conditions expected of me were really in my best interest. I had been living with the simple, childlike logic of following rules = needs met. I never stopped to get curious and ask questions like:

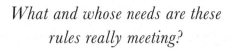

*What and whose needs are these
rules really meeting?*

*How exactly are they meeting mine?*

*Could there be other means of meeting my
needs that I would actually enjoy?*

Nope, these questions didn't come to the surface at all. I would remain identified with being the Obedient One, the Workhorse, and the Responsible One, just following orders to prove my worth and get by in the world. It wasn't until much later in life that I was able to look back and understand whose needs I was really meeting. I could eventually see more clearly how the Student-Athlete definitely met the needs of the university. I realize this would be a more impactful statement if I were a football or basketball student-athlete. According to *Business Insider,* track and field still bring in a profit for National Collegiate Athletic Association (NCAA) Division 1 schools.[1]

Another *Business Insider* article, "Chart Shows How Little of College Sports Revenues Goes to the Athletes," shows that money brought in by the athletic departments clearly benefits and works to meet the school's needs.[2]

I wish I had stopped to take ownership of my own decisions and asked myself, *Which of my needs were actually being met when I kept that track and field scholarship even though I already had a full academic scholarship? And in so doing, did I choose to sacrifice the time I ideally could have used to explore what I really enjoyed, which would have helped me decide what I really wanted to do with my future?*

Similar to the time of that West Point appointment, I again had not stopped to consider that the track scholarship money could have gone to someone else who actually LOVED track and field and possibly that scholarship would have been their only way to get to attend the university. Meanwhile, I could have been exploring and pursuing my dreams while still getting my education paid for with the academic scholarship. I also suspect that had I learned how to stop and listen to Lou back then, she would have helped show me this new effortless, buildable, enjoyable approach was not just for endurance training on the track.

None of this crossed my mind at that time. I was consumed by my subconscious need to feel safe in a scary world the only way I knew how and to avoid more abandonment.

The other interesting thing about our personal stories and the nature of our adopted personas is that they do somehow work for us, even if only temporarily. I've learned we stay committed to our fear-based stories, even if they aren't authentic to us, because they provide a deeper secondary gain. I went on to become the track team's co-captain in my senior year.

For many years following graduation, I still held some of the track records I set during that time. When I would visit Dad in the summers long after I had graduated, he would still be watching the home videos of me "coming up from behind" to win races. One of his favorite Hollywood movies, when we were young, was *The Black Stallion* and I really think his home movies of us playing sports gave him that same thrill as this Oscar-nominated film. I was thankful to have remained in his good graces, and at the time it seemed perfectly worth the cost.

# CHAPTER 5

# *The Doctor*

Still on the autopilot of following the rules laid out for me, I graduated from the university, married my athlete boyfriend, and headed off to medical school. As the Doctor, it was easy to rationalize abandoning myself. It seemed to be woven into the "house rules" of medicine that this was a house built on self-sacrifice. In the medical field, self-abandonment is seen as honorable and it pays six figures, so it's no wonder so many of us lined up to leave ourselves behind. As the Doctor, it seemed like I had joined a league of professional abandoners.

Now before I go on, please allow me to stop here and make something very clear. I believe the medical field is truly honorable and the sacrifices made by physicians, nurses, and the essential workers that support them in the name of helping the rest of us and the greater good is extraordinary. In this year of COVID-19, the courageousness and sacrifice has been more visible than usual. I'd like to simply remind you here that you are still reading my story, and my own perspective on my personal life. I was not equipped with the knowledge of how vital it is to refill my tank once I got to the point of empty. More accurately, while I was in the medical field, I was not even aware of when I was running on empty. Obviously, there are so many medical professionals who both know how to serve and to succeed without self-neglect. This chapter is for those who can appreciate that I was coming from a place where neglecting myself, blind obedience, and self-sacrifice was all I knew. For me, the medical field was the prime training ground to reinforce and perfect those skills.

As young doctors, our journey began with a white coat ceremony where we recited the Hippocratic Oath. We were taught the notion of *non-maleficence* (or in other words, "First, do no harm"). The irony was that the system itself modeled behaviors that could harm us in the long run. A lot of time has elapsed since I went through medical school, but I'd still be very surprised if the focus has shifted to teaching doctors how to take care of themselves first.

*From a place of fullness, we are always
better equipped to take care of others.*

You've undoubtedly heard the following types of stories, and unfortunately, I can personally attest these were true at that time.

- It was recommended when I went through training never to have surgery in the afternoon, as it's very likely your doctor will be overtired from potentially having been up all night saving someone else's life and running on one or two hours of sleep.

- Doctors often spent seven days a week being a doctor, if you include their on-call hours as well as their documentation and administrative duties. Everything else in their lives is expected to be second, including family, friends, leisure, and self-care.

- As suspected, when I was in medical training, based on the number of people we knew or knew of, it has now been officially confirmed in 2018 that "one doctor commits suicide in the U.S. every day—the highest suicide rate of any profession." [1]

As the Doctor, I felt guilty for even considering taking a vacation or thinking about saying no to staying at work a few extra hours longer to help a patient who had walked in sick at the end of the day, in spite of the fact we (and our support staff) had already put in a full twelve-hour shift. And usually because of that guilt, and because this was the way of those that came before us in the name of dedication to helping others, we would skip vacations we were entitled to, and we would all stay several hours longer.

Hopefully, by now our medical system's training ground is catching on to the irony in this approach and trying other, maybe more commonsense approaches, such as overlapping shifts or investing in extra support staff to cover unforeseen events. This newer approach would be more ideal than asking loyal doctors and support staff to honorably sacrifice their own health or asking their families to sacrifice quality time with their loved ones. And too often, once an overstretched doctor and her support staff do get home to rest and recover, they are too tired to give quality attention to whomever is there waiting for them.

In my personal experience, commonly there was usually no one waiting for those overstretched medical providers as they hadn't had any time to invest in developing actual relationships. We would have big, beautiful houses or luxury apartments because medicine pays very well, but too often we'd spent the majority of our young adult lives going from nonstop studying to nonstop working, without ever dedicating any real time to developing the skills required to sustain a meaningful relationship. I've witnessed many doctors who live to work, work, and work some more, attend conferences, maybe even do some volunteering, while their personal lives are limited to an occasional date or one-night stand, and while their big, beautiful house or luxury apartment goes empty and is void of life.

The area of self-harm that I am most personally acquainted with is the financial debt that most doctors live with for far too long after graduating school. Even with very high salaries, many doctors don't actually pay off their medical school loans until their forties or even well into their fifties. One of the heads of the Family Medicine Department at the hospital where I was assigned a clinical rotation once told our team, "Yeah, you'll need to get used to the debt. It is what it is."

As our $150,000-plus medical school debt was staring us down, there was very little preparation for the additional costs of malpractice insurance, medical equipment overhead, or the dues and fees for continuing education expenses and certifications waiting for us once we graduated. I would be very surprised if this has changed much either. Just this year, while riding the train from Westchester County to Manhattan, I saw a printed bank advertisement on the wall of my train car that read: "Who knew that MD stood for Major Debt?"

*Living with debt as a way of life, instead of being taught to live from fullness and abundance and then giving from the overflow, was one of the many "house rules" I would forget to question as the Doctor.*

It was very real for me that we were missing actual role models in medicine that could pave a healthier way instead of reinforcing this self-harm/self-sacrifice/embrace-debt paradigm. There were the multimillionaire specialists who at the end of the day had a net income less than the blue-collar counterparts they passed in the grocery store. Our predecessors taught us by example to live above our means, buy the most elite toys, and engage in risky business ventures. They did their best to cover their debts with an extra surgery here or a few more procedures there.

There were very few predecessors in my world stopping to ask questions like:

*What if that side venture falls through or an unforeseen event occurs, and I cannot do those extra procedures to cover my costs anymore?*

*What happens when the stress of it all leads to an increase in using addictive substances to numb those* what-ifs? *Maybe the anesthesia cart gives me easy access to ketamine, or the nurse could just call in a personal narcotic refill for me this one time.*

*What happens when I've spent so many hours at work and that sexy, young trainee, who makes sure her thong always peeks out above her scrubs when she is bent over, or that hot, new doctor who keeps telling stories about how his wife nags him that he's never home, starts showing me extra attention and that hospital on-call suite is just conveniently down the hall?*

What I witnessed happen all too often was the perfect prescription for abandoned bodies, abandoned ethics, and abandoned homes. Luckily, witnessing the violations of ethics at least sparked the Obedient One in me to ask my own questions and not so blindly follow the crowd.

And, just to be clear, these providers, although modeling self-abandonment, were also very good at the practice of medicine and at caring for their patients. They literally saved lives almost daily. They were honored and revered. They sometimes did incredible feats with almost superhuman skill and precision in the midst of emergencies and crises. Knowing you made a difference in other people's lives and knowing you've saved lives is honorable. But if you aren't taking care of yourself, this way of life is rarely sustainable for those involved.

Even the best of the self-sacrificing, honorable doctors I knew ended up with two or three marriages or had children who barely knew them. We may have been enjoying the fruits of our labor, but at what cost?

Again, please remember I am not saying this is everyone in medicine. I am not speaking to the healthcare providers who had their shit together even in medical school and knew the basics for building a happy life while also caring for their patients. I am speaking to those like me who learned how to perfect our already preconditioned tendencies toward over-functioning, self-sacrificing, and indebtedness because we came from homes filled with addictive tendencies and/or loneliness and depression. I am speaking to whomever found themselves in a professional environment that was the perfect breeding ground to lead them to further self-abandonment and neglect. For me, that just happened to be the medical world.

As the Doctor, I worked seven days a week, rarely took vacations, and was staring down twenty years of debt. I was continually sleep deprived and missing out on most holidays, birthdays, and family gatherings in the name of being the Doctor and taking care of my patients. Because of my habits formed in track and field, I did at least find time to exercise and made meager attempts at building a relationship with my husband who had gone on to become a professional athlete after college. But I hope you have now noticed the absence of a certain little one's perspective.

Yes, that's right. Lou would not be heard at all while I was the Doctor. I was now an adult with huge adult responsibilities. As a married adult, I also had to figure out who exactly I would be in the relationship. I knew the rules for being the

Doctor, the Workhorse, and the Obedient One; what they all shared at their core was a strong sense of responsibility. Lou's childhood dreams and desires seemed to be irrelevant now. The Responsible One was who made the most sense to take the lead in my relationships.

# CHAPTER 6

# *The Responsible One*

As you may remember, I (Lou) longed to have that dream home life. The kind where there was unconditional love and the people in the home were curious about each other, interested in the details of each other's lives, and wanted to help create a safe and nurturing environment in which everyone could blossom to their fullest desires and potential. With no idea where to start, I left college still determined to create that home life for myself one day. My eyes were set on the high school boyfriend. We had gone from high school to university together, and we then married right after I graduated with the plan to one day start a family together. Being the Obedient One, I waited until marriage to lose my virginity with him (finally) and I believed all would finally be safe and happily ever after. We were following the "rules," so it should have been simple, right?

This is how I remember my first attempt at a real relationship. My ex, let's call him Mr. Ballplayer, may have a completely different version of those years, but that would make sense as we spent the majority of those years living apart. At the university, my boyfriend was on the varsity baseball team. Professional scouts started tracking his performance. He was known in school to be a realistic candidate for being signed by a pro team, and he was clearly excited to live out his dreams of playing baseball. When the opportunity presented itself to sign with a pro team, he understandably seized the opportunity. We squeezed in a wedding between training and tryouts. Then, without a honeymoon, we both went straight on to what we from the outside appeared to know how to do best—being the oldest child in a household who lived to earn our respective dad's approval.

That may actually have been the biggest thing we had in common. We were both known as honest, well-liked, athletically gifted people. In hindsight, I believe we were also similarly afraid of the big, scary world and neither of us were excited at the idea of getting out there alone. Both of our fathers could be heard by many talking about how accomplished their oldest child was at what he/she did. In our reality, though, neither of our fathers actually knew much about what was really going on in our personal lives.

Mr. Ballplayer's father seemed, from my view, only to be interested in talking about statistics from the most recent ball game and then hanging up. They may have spoken hours about other things when I was just not there to see it. But I don't think they did. I used to point out repeatedly that at least my father would tell me he loved me before hanging up when I called him. Mr. Ballplayer's rebuttal would be that at least his father picked up the phone to call him regularly, while with mine, I was always the one required to place the call or there would likely be no call at all. Mr. Ballplayer was right. Dad rarely picked up the phone to call me on his own initiative, but Dad's excuse was that he didn't want to "disturb all of my doctoring work." Mr. Ballplayer was also right in that there could be weeks to months between calls sometimes with Dad because I was so absorbed in my medical training.

The other trait we seemed to have in common was our commitment to our respective work. My medical training required a seven-days-per-week commitment from me and countless sleepless nights. Meanwhile, Mr. Ballplayer's athletic career required countless hours of traveling, sleeping in hotels, and a commitment to hours of daily practice to refine his skills. We technically did not live in the same place for more than six months out of the year and this was usually only during the off-season. For me, our marriage often felt like I lived with a stranger.

Eventually, I'd gradually get to know Mr. Ballplayer again, we'd start to sync up our rhythms, but by then it would be time for him to head out on the road again and off he'd go. Even though we wore wedding bands, we lived very separate lives while we trained for our respective "oldest child in Dad's good graces" careers.

I do specifically recall Mr. Ballplayer's father questioning why we would want to move forward in the relationship if we'd just be living apart. Because of this, he essentially did not approve of our decision to marry. We, as youth often do, ignored his sage advice and married anyway.

*As it is with 20-20 hindsight, there were gifts right in front of us that we couldn't see.*

My father had professional sports experience and could have easily guided Mr. Ballplayer to choose steps that did not require learning as many things the hard way. Likewise, his father understood the medical field and could have easily guided me to make choices that did not require me learning as many things the hard way either. We were young with blinders on; yet another thing we had in common.

And there I was, in a relationship but still spending most of my free time alone and crying a lot. Hmmm, I recall another Lana crying a lot in her marriage, too. *Nooo, it's not the same, he's nothing like Dad,* I'd reassure myself. I just had not yet asked myself if I was anything like her.

I thought I had made sure my significant other would be the opposite of Dad: a completely different race and a completely different personality. Yes, he might have an occasional temper as many people do, but in comparison to Dad's, his flareups were more like tantrums and certainly never as scary. But he did indeed become a professional athlete like Dad, and I would later learn that, like Dad, he was a similar magnet for the female persuasion. Who knew groupies were a real thing?

I had been crying myself to sleep at night since the second night of married life (when I learned that he had changed our plans last minute and we would actually be living above someone's garage in steaming hot Orlando, Florida, and stumbling upon four-inch hairy Florida spiders on the walls, instead of living by the beach in Naples as we previously agreed). I felt hopeless because I was convinced, as the Responsible One, that since I'd made my bed, now I was doomed to lie in it. Divorce was not an option in the rulebook I was still following, so I hid our dirty laundry. I told no one, I shoved my feelings down, and I stayed quiet just as I had learned to do in the past.

What the Responsible One brought to the table was not only making sure I followed the rules but also the belief that I was responsible for helping everyone else do the same. The Responsible One was born the morning after Mom died. The moment I told myself it was time to take care of my younger sister, I gave the Responsible One her mission and she chose to accept it. Her mission was to keep not only me but everyone around me from feeling pain, and to keep everybody safe from perceived danger. I then set out to accomplish this by preventing people from making what I believed were poor choices. I determined which choices were poor by measuring them against whether or not they broke the "rules," since clearly breaking the rules meant impending danger and pain. So, for a seven-year-old mind, this mission and proposed plan of execution made perfect sense. I then quickly and masterfully began to perfect these skills.

If any of this is resonating with you, you are probably all too familiar with the qualities of my Responsible One, but for those of you who are unfamiliar, please allow me to get you acquainted. You may know your own Responsible One as any of these: the Peacekeeping One, the Enabling One, the Reliable one, the Helping One, the Over-functioning One, or my favorite, the I-Might-As-Well-Do-It-Myself One (since then I can be sure it will be done right). If you were a "parentified child," you likely came to embody your own version of the Responsible One.

As a child, if I, the Obedient One, was getting all of my designated chores done and doing all of my schoolwork on time, the Responsible One would then step up and notice that it was almost time for Dad to get home from work and my sister had not yet finished hers. My sister would sometimes literally be nowhere to be found and I knew all hell would break loose when Dad got home if the chores were not done. The Responsible One would kick into a new gear and finish all my sister's chores, too, so that none of us (especially not Lou) needed to feel the wrath of Dad.

In other words, as the Responsible One, I used my superpowers to sense potential danger and protect myself and others. In the above instance, Dad would walk in happy as a clam because there was a clean house and dinner on the table. Mission accomplished! All was still safe in our world. Danger prevented.

When we got older, my sister eventually disclosed to me that I had been so predictable that all she needed to do was wait just long enough until I would reach my threshold and do all of her chores for her. She said she did it all of the time and I never noticed.

Other times, since I was the one responsible for getting straight-As on every report card, my next step would be to make sure to show Dad my report card first to get him into a good mood and help soften the blow from seeing my sister's report card with Cs, or sometimes Ds. I knew mission was accomplished again when, instead of yelling, he would only say, "It's OK, she'll do better next time."

As I grew up, this might look like me literally fainting if I somehow had a momentary lapse of judgment and realized I was caught breaking the rules. One such time was when I was so jealous of the more privileged kids whose parents drove us to and from Sunday school that, when they stopped at the store to buy candy, and we couldn't afford it, I suddenly remembered the coins in my pocket. I had also somehow failed to remember that those coins were supposed to be for the church offering plate, and used them to buy candy instead. When we got home, while mindlessly sucking on a lollipop, Dad asked who gave me the candy, and it hit me like a ton of bricks that I had just used God's tithe money to buy candy. Then down I went. I passed out cold, simply because my Responsible One was flooded with overwhelming shock at how irresponsible I had been and what impending danger must be awaiting this travesty.

Passing out luckily softened Dad's mood (he found it kind of comical), so it turned out the Responsible One still knew how to save me from his "wrath."

In my teenage years, being responsible looked like me being the one who thought to shut the windows so the neighbors couldn't hear as Dad shouted about something, and hopefully prevent them from calling the cops on us for disturbing the peace or other imagined potentially dangerous altercations. Or it looked like me being the one to be scolded for being a "bad influence" on my younger sister (although you already know my version of "bad" was probably laughable by most standards). And on those occasions when I could not succeed in preventing the danger, it was the unspoken agreement that it was still my responsibility to be the one who comforted and nursed our pets, or sometimes Dad's current girlfriend.

As the Responsible One, I was predictable in that everyone in my world knew they could always count on me. Since I was so great at preventing some unforeseen danger, I would dole out advice to anyone with confidence. Friends, patients, and colleagues would continually thank me for how much I made things easier for them in one way or another. As the Doctor, if my office staff needed to leave without finishing all the insurance forms or calling back a patient waiting on test results, I would, of course, volunteer to stay at the office until everything was done. And while married to the professional ballplayer, I thought it was my responsibility as the good wife to take out the maximum loans allowed for medical school knowing I'd be using it to cover not only my share of expenses but also the majority of expenses that he incurred.

My Responsible One's ability to predict and prevent danger felt like I was a superhero. I used this power well when I was responsible for the well-being of my patients as the Doctor. However, the shadow side of astutely predicting and preventing danger was that it reinforced a growing notion in me that I actually knew what was "right" for everyone.

As a child armed with Bible verses in my head, I would reprimand Dad for his drinking and womanizing (initially only in my head, but later on aloud as well), and then I would explain how I'd better go pray for him at church. Or in my relationship, if you were a fly on the wall, you might find me similarly shaming my professional-athlete-roommate-with-a-wedding-band for not making what were clearly to me the "right" decisions, like keeping up with his half of paying the bills or lecturing on what I deemed was or wasn't appropriate husband behavior with other women. And with him, these judgments and reprimands were most certainly always very out loud. I must have skipped the class in Superheroine Academy that explained that superheroes would do well to learn to only use their powers for good.

If you've ever over-functioned as the Responsible One, then I don't need to explain in much detail how exhausting life can get doing everything for yourself and everyone else. And as the Obedient One, everything also had to be done with a smile. I tried for as long as I could to keep up the façade that, as the good, well-liked, happy Christian couple I thought we were, we were doing just fine. The truth was, I was exhausted, and I resented over-functioning. I somehow survived four years of medical school and three years of residency with my head down, focused on only work and household chores, all the while pushing down my feelings of pain, anger, and loneliness.

I rationalized that the exhaustion and running on empty were due to choosing a life in the medical field. When the day finally came that Mr. Ballplayer let me know that he wasn't going to stay for the marital counseling we had scheduled and that instead he must return to chasing his dreams no matter what the cost, I supported his decision to leave. But I also asked that he not come back. Somewhere inside, I knew for me it meant it was time to finally have a break from the self-inflicted heaviness of carrying a magnitude of responsibilities that were not all my own.

Unfortunately, it's hard to teach a Pavlovian dog such as myself new tricks, so it wasn't long before I was up to my familiar habitual ways of enabling other people and over-functioning. I jumped right back in headfirst into causing my own self-inflicted suffering in the name of avoiding abandonment and finding someone who'd approve of me.

# CHAPTER 7

# My Angel and Teacher, Theodore Bear

Speaking of dogs, before I dive into my story of hitting rock bottom, in which my dog Teddy played a key role, I'm reminded of a trick to clue in to how someone is showing up in life or how he'll/she'll be as a future partner. When in doubt, ask his/her pet.

> *How people relate to animals will tell*
> *you how they relate to themselves and*
> *how they show up in relationships.*

I wish someone had explained this to me way back when, as maybe it could have triggered me sooner to do some introspection. Maybe it would have helped me to see red flags that I couldn't quite see clearly at the time.

For instance, Dad's relationship with animals varied; it had the same extremes and intensity as it did when he was with his family members. Some of our favorite times as kids were when he would take us horseback riding and I would watch the connection between him and the horse he rode with awe. He didn't seem to need to do much at all to get the horse to go where he wanted, and they both seemed to enjoy the full-on gallop down the path and through the farm. They looked like they were both happy to be free. Or our dog Yaro, the Old English sheepdog that Lou would cuddle with, who was so gentle and passive. Yaro had the obedience game down to a science. I never once saw Dad raise his voice or a hand toward her. She never needed a leash, and Dad could tell her to go find us outside in other children's yards when it was it was time for supper. She'd come.

But then, other times, our pets shook in fear of Dad's presence as I sometimes did. In theory, if any of his girlfriends had stopped to ask me about Dad's demeanor with animals, she could have potentially saved herself from heartbreak. But which of us have the wherewithal to inquire or even to heed early warning signs when we think we know what love is?

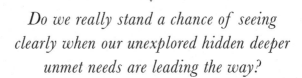

*Do we really stand a chance of seeing*
*clearly when our unexplored hidden deeper*
*unmet needs are leading the way?*

It is always easier in hindsight to examine signs that were there all along. It only gets easier after the fact to recognize those Diamonds and Pearls. When I take a trip down memory lane now and look back at my exes and their interactions with their pets, certain things start to make perfect sense. Mr. Ballplayer grew up with two dogs of his own, but he and his family kept them outdoors most of the time. This was in stark contrast to my family's "emmeshed" approach of allowing our dogs to sleep inside, and even in bed with us. On one occasion in the winter, Mr. Ballplayer and my dad's dog went on a cross-country skiing jaunt through a wooded park near our home. When they returned, the dog had a laceration across his front leg. I imagine the dog ran in front of the ski blade and accidentally sliced his leg. But even though it was the dog's accident, *so irresponsible* was all I could think about Mr. Ballplayer for not being "responsible enough" to protect the dog from any danger; and interestingly, like a curious déjà vu, there I was, nursing another pet.

Another time, while I was busy with my residency training, Mr. Ballplayer thought he would make a kind gesture and cheer me up by bringing home a puppy from the local mall. I believe he genuinely was intending to be thoughtful, and I don't think he could have predicted how I reacted. But I was absolutely livid. "This is a living creature! It needs care! It needs someone to be responsible for its welfare. When you go back to your sports training camp and I am working all hours of the night at the hospital, who will be responsible?!? How inconsiderate! Take it back!" I demanded. (Yeah, I know. The Responsible One in the dog pack can be quite a "bitch.")

Inside, my stomach turned, as if I'd vomit at what I was thinking about this poor puppy and what seemed to me at the time to be an expression of utter carelessness for its life. I couldn't even look at the puppy, as I was certain I'd fall in love with it and would then never have the strength to let it go. "Didn't he realize I couldn't possibly be responsible for one single thing more since I was already overextended waaay past my limit?!?" Being waaay overextended was also precisely my excuse for my putting off having kids. I finally realized that since he was gone roughly six-plus months of the year and I was in medical training seven days a week, who would possibly be responsible for actually raising these kids I thought I wanted so badly? I refused to have children grow up in an empty home, isolated and alone. From my view, I wouldn't allow a dog to suffer like that either.

On my insistence, we returned the puppy the same day, but when we called the store a couple of days later to see if they'd found it a new home yet, they regretfully informed us it had died of parvovirus, a common puppy mill illness. I couldn't even wrap my head around the thought of a puppy dying, and worse yet, potentially dying in our home because we bought it from a company that engaged in shady practices. On top of it all, thoughts raced in my head that somehow now I was also responsible for its death, too. It was almost unbearable.

*In hindsight, overextending myself gave me a convenient excuse to be too busy to*

*really enjoy life or to work on improving
the quality of my relationships.*

I wasn't ready yet to lay down the duties of the over-functioning Responsible One, who essentially judged others as less than capable and who thought she knew what was "right" for them. I wasn't ready yet to be vulnerable and trust another soul. I wasn't ready yet to gift someone with the opportunity of rising to the occasion, of embracing our personal power, and of seeing where that could take us. Thank you, Mr. Ballplayer, for your patience back then. I apologize for enabling and trying to be responsible for what was yours. I am sorry for not allowing a space for you to "step up to the plate" and own your shine.

When I finally did get a dog of my own, it was because I chose to "rescue" one from Dad. This dog came into the picture because Mr. Ballplayer and I thought we were finally at a place in our lives that we could successfully care for a dog, and so we went looking at a litter of black Labrador retriever/German shepherd mixes on a nearby farm. But before they were even eight weeks old and ready for us to take one home, we canceled the pickup. Mr. Ballplayer was leaving yet again for his summer ball season and I again didn't want to raise a pup alone.

Soon after, Dad came to town to visit and inquired why I had no dog. He then begged me all weekend to take him to see the puppies on the farm, which I reluctantly, but of course obediently, did. The next thing I knew, Dad was driving back home with the alpha puppy of the pack, Theodore Bear, or

Teddy, for short, in the back seat of his car. I did not have a good feeling about this adoption at all.

Needless to say, the novelty of having a puppy wore off quickly for Dad. My sister and I both would try to take the puppy away from him for the weekend, if just to give him a break. We could tell the puppy was miserable there with him. The puppy was locked in a crate most of the time, and all Dad seemed to do was complain about how he wouldn't obey him as our first dog, Yaro, did. When my sister and I took the pup to her apartment to babysit, he would proceed to tear apart everything in sight. The insides of her pillows would look like clouds on the floor. There were little teeth marks on everything wooded within reach, and shoes weren't safe if left on the floor.

After about one year, I couldn't take the thought of that puppy living with Dad anymore, especially the picture in my head of him spending the majority of his time in a crate instead of running around free and having fun. I finally told Dad, "Please just give me the dog already," and I took Teddy home to my apartment to live with me.

I thought about getting rid of Teddy, but by then he was so unsocialized and misbehaving that I was afraid if I turned him in to an animal shelter he would be put to sleep. So I was determined to find a way to give him a proper home on my own. Around this time, I was still adjusting to being single again, living alone, and still in the middle of my residency, which meant I was still working six-plus days a week and thirty- to thirty-six-hour shifts. I definitely did not have a routine that a dog could follow.

I tried pet sitters and doggie daycares, and Teddy was kicked out of them all. When I couldn't find someone brave enough to watch him, I would leave potty training mats all over the floor and extra bowls of food and water, hoping he'd remember his early puppy days and go on the training pads. To no one's surprise, I'd come home to find he'd torn apart the carpet, pooped on the couch, pulled down my blinds, and was sitting in the middle of the floor, ears back, looking innocent but waiting to see how I would react. I couldn't even bring myself to get mad at him. First, he was too cute. More importantly, I felt completely responsible.

Even though I didn't have a clue how to help him, I must somehow have been convinced that I was the only one in all of New York State willing to care for him. Of course I felt that way—the Responsible One was responsible for everyone and everything, right?

Anyone watching me could have easily seen the direct correlation between how I approached my relationship with Teddy and how I was showing up in my own life. Anyone watching could have seen this except me, that is. I'm now sure Lou saw it, but I was long past listening to Lou.

This was now right about the time I took an interest in a certain unnamed someone in town. Like me, he had just ended a long-term relationship and he seemed well liked, intelligent, and responsible. Once we started to spend time together, he introduced me to his parents surprisingly quickly. Our first "date" was at an air show and his parents were there, too. He was an only child and his parents seemed like they were genuinely interested in his life and proud of him. They also seemed to take a genuine interest in me. *Wow*, I'd think. *Both parents still together in a picture-perfect home, and he understands life as a busy professional, and he also loves dogs! Is it possible that I could have found someone so "perfect"?*

But remember, if someone could have given me the insight to look at how I was caring for my dog, Teddy, as a reflection of what was going on with me, it would have been priceless information. I started spending more time away from Teddy as I was working my usual long hours at the hospital and napping on the couch with my new romantic interest at his place, only to wake up a couple of hours later, realizing I had completely lost track of time. Essentially, while I was basking in the approval of a man, Teddy was sitting home alone again, I'm sure feeling neglected . . . and dare I say, abandoned. This is still painful even now to write. I have so much compassion, love, and reverence for the gift of that dog.

At least I knew that once I graduated from the medical residency, I'd have a more regular schedule as the Doctor, and I promised myself I would use this transition time to take better care of Teddy. I rented a small house with a big backyard. I added a fenced-in area and attached it to the house and got permission from the landlord to add a doggy door that opened to this outdoor pen. Teddy would have the ability to make choices: He could choose to bask in the sun outside or go indoors to get food and avoid inclement weather. Teddy seemed to appreciate these changes and choices and responded positively, although gradually, to my newfound interest in him.

He was also growing up to be a strong dog, looking more like a handsome, but intimidating, German shepherd than a docile black Lab. Even the staff at every vet office would stop and point him out of the crowd of dogs in the waiting room and comment, "Wow, that's a good-looking dog." It's funny, he reminded me a lot of my dad in that way. Everywhere I went, my female friends and perfect strangers would find it necessary to come over and say things to Dad like, "I don't mean to be forward, but you smell amazing," or (to me) "Your dad is so good looking—how old is he?" To prevent people from succumbing to their handsome spell, both Teddy and my dad would actually have benefited from wearing a sign around their necks that read, "Beware, I might bite."

Teddy did, indeed, try to bite strangers that didn't pass his sniff test or who made sudden movements in our direction. He barked at and chased off both the mailman and the cable man. Before he finally successfully bit someone, I paid for sessions with a dog behavioral therapist. The specialist taught me about separation anxiety, which explained why Teddy had previously torn apart my apartment and acted out when strangers came to the door. He explained that a lot of Teddy's territorial behaviors were because he was reading MY energy around others. That threw me, but it made perfect sense. Teddy's bark was impressive, and when he was on guard, his look usually gave even dog lovers a second thought at approaching him.

The specialist went on to explain that Teddy sensed when I was even the slightest bit fearful on the inside, even if I was just afraid of what Teddy might do to a stranger. Teddy, in turn, would respond to my energy by stepping up to be the alpha dog in our pack, since I wasn't. Teddy was showing me how afraid of the big scary world little Lou still was. Unknown to me, Teddy and I were actually trading positions as pack leader, depending on the situation.

As I eventually introduced my new male interest to our pack, again, I do wish I had paid closer attention to the *Ask Your Pet* theory. There was one time, within a few months of our dating, that I needed to ask this new interest (let's call him Mr. CEO) to take Teddy on a walk for me since I wouldn't be getting out of the office until pretty late. When I got home, Teddy was there along with a note to call Mr. CEO ASAP. Mr. CEO was in the emergency room and they were deciding the next steps for his dog bite. To make a long story short, Mr. CEO explained that for unclear reasons Teddy had firmly and definitively bitten down onto his thumb and punctured it with his teeth.

When Mr. CEO returned from the ER, he admitted that he wasn't angry at Teddy, and in fact, stated he partially blamed himself (which the Responsible One in me loved to hear). After that, Teddy and Mr. CEO were able to take many long walks in the woods behind his parents' place, playing endless games of fetch, and other made-up games that involved a ball. When watching the two of them, I would think they could have been siblings. And Teddy seemed to have given me the green light to add Mr. CEO to our pack, but only as his play-mate. Meanwhile, I was still trying my best to hold the position as official pack leader and carry the responsibility of meeting Teddy's needs along with my own.

I can still remember, like yesterday, the exact moment when the dynamic between us changed from pack leader and dog to one of mutual respect and a true relationship. My schedule was becoming more routine and predictable. Teddy, in turn, was becoming less reactive. He would even let some strangers pet him. I still tried to get to church regularly on Sundays, and Teddy started being able to tell which days were weekdays vs. weekends. On weekdays, I sat on the end of my bed to put on my scrub pants, which was Teddy's cue to get up, stretch, and go outside with me to do his business before I left for work. Sundays, on the other hand, I would put on a dress and return after an hour of being away instead of being away all day long.

One Sunday, I noticed he didn't get out of his bed at all. I tried to encourage him to get up by saying, "Come on, Ted, you know the drill. Let's go so I can take you outside before I go to church. Come on now, or I'm going to be late." I patted my leg as a signal for him to come. But Teddy just lay there curled in a comfy ball on his bed looking up at me. I knew I would be back in an hour, so I said, "Fine, suit yourself, I'll be back."

When I got home an hour later, Teddy slowly got up off of his bed, stretched in his version of Downward Dog, walked over to the door, and stood ready for me to take him outside. He repeated this behavior the following Sunday, so I knew he'd just taught me that this would become our new Sunday routine. From then on, I wouldn't even bother trying to wake him if it was a Sunday. Teddy simply preferred to sleep in an extra hour on the weekends and I was fine with that!

The exact turning point I was referring to earlier occurred on a more hectic morning when I was headed to work. I was getting Teddy's leash ready but had agreed to let him head outside before me. Our routine was that he would stay in front of the house and wait for me to put his leash on. Then we would walk down the hill beside the house to get to the backyard. He must've seen something, maybe a small animal along the side of the house, because Teddy darted off and out of sight instead of waiting for me. I wouldn't have minded this as much if we were behind Mr. CEO's parent's place where there were miles of woods, but my rental home was surrounded by busy streets with traffic and the dog could easily have been hit by a car. Not to mention the stress this was creating by making me late for work.

I started to chase after Teddy, but quickly realized he was way too far ahead. I just stood still, dropping my arms to my sides, holding the empty leash in my hand. Leaning my head back while looking up at the sky and feeling completely defeated, I said under my breath and on the exhale, "Ohhh Teddy." The volume of my voice couldn't have been more than a whisper, and his back was to me as he ran in full stride, chasing something across the neighboring backyard in the distance. But in the exact moment I gave up, he stopped on a dime and looked back at me. To my astonishment, he came running back to me, sat down next to my leg, and leaned his head against the hand that was holding the leash, as if to say, "Here, we're in this together. We'll have fun chasing things when you get home."

I was in shock. This animal was truly amazing.

*It was fascinating to feel what it was like to have*
*another being attuned to me, sensing my energy,*
*and interested in looking out for me this time.*

From that moment forward, Teddy rarely needed to wear a
leash unless we were in an unknown area. He responded to my
hand gestures, or even at times just to my certain look or a nod.
I made a point to pay more attention by checking in with him
and reading what he might need. Teddy was teaching me some
basic relationship skills I had been lacking.

I may have been a slow learner, but I was learning, nonetheless. Fourteen-plus years went by and I can happily say Teddy
had a really good life for about twelve of those years. At ten
years old, I watched Teddy climb Blue Mountain in Saranac,
New York, and he playfully darted up almost the entire mountain like a puppy. As he passed strangers on the hike, he let
them pet him and he really seemed to be in his element. He
loved the outdoors, especially the woods, water, and snow. We
went on hiking trips and outings as often as possible. But eventually, Teddy and I needed to start trading pack leader roles
again. I had hit a plateau in my School of Life education.

Specifically, I had not yet learned how to focus these
"checking-in" efforts and the new paying-attention skill set toward myself. I was good at checking in and attuning myself to
Teddy's needs, but was still abandoning my own. There were
nights that I would stay awake on the couch, crying in despair

from relationship woes, and Teddy would find it necessary to jump up on the couch next to me. He'd position himself by sitting up tall with his chest puffed out and facing outward into the empty room. He'd make sure his back was to me, and that I was behind him as he protected me from the empty room while I was in my most vulnerable state. It was his offering to me, even if just for that moment, to take on being the Responsible One and be my protector while I let it all go and just cried.

# Nowhere Else to Run (aka at Rock Bottom)

Even though I was learning a lot about relationships during my time with Teddy, the bulk of my time with humans, for essentially thirteen-plus years, was blindly spent living on auto-pilot as the Doctor and the Responsible One. The growth I was making with Teddy, actually learning what it feels like to have "someone" attuned to me and paying attention as Ted would, did not translate, unfortunately, into me learning to be attuned and paying attention to myself.

*My focus was still completely outside myself.*
*I was always looking for external validation*
*to give me what may as well have been*

*"approval" for my very existence. My value*
*was still only what others said it was.*

As long as I was meeting the expectations and conditions required of the Doctor or the over-functioning Responsible One, I believed I was OK. However, I now know that basing your value and worth on your external circumstances and other people's expectations is very fragile ground to stand on.

For instance, I was certain that Mr. CEO appreciated my physical appearance. I had an athletic body and long, dark hair (albeit straightened and not natural). I was certain he valued my pretty face (whenever it wasn't breaking out in the intermittent cystic acne from my bottled-up stress and anger). I believed, because of outside opinions, that these assets were valuable. But as I got older, and I got the impression that I was being compared to younger girls with better skin and naturally silky, straight hair and everything else that's traditionally appealing about twenty-somethings that late thirty-somethings no longer possess, my tiny sense of self-value diminished.

I was also convinced in my mind that I was only valued for my over-functioning superpowers. When Mr. CEO and I eventually moved in together after ten years of dating, and though we were both busy with our careers, there was an unspoken expectation that I would cook dinner, clean the house, and act as a buffer between him and his family. Or I should say, this was my understanding of what was expected.

To be clear, Mr. CEO never actually laid out such an expectation. This was my own interpretation of what I should do since I was feeling grateful and had a sense of obligation that he was allowing me to live in his condo without contributing to the mortgage.

I'm sure I've mentioned this before, but it is my belief that no one does anything without gaining something from it, even if that something is not a conscious gain. For me, with Mr. CEO, I gained glimpses of that dream family life with both parents still living happily together I had always hoped to experience. Every vacation during the thirteen years we were "a couple," with the exception of our first vacation, was spent with either his parents or his extended family.

Many of his family members, especially his parents, spoke on the phone with me often, and we had genuine, meaningful conversations. We were curious about each other's lives and we talked over dinner. We cooked together and I learned their family recipes for almost everything from marinara sauce to an aunt's secret cookie recipe. I truly enjoyed their company, and I believed they enjoyed mine, too. Meanwhile, while I enjoyed his parents' company, Mr. CEO often seemed to most enjoy the chance to relax on the couch or disappear into his laptop. He also seemed to enjoy helping his father outside in the yard or to run errands. But with time, I realized I had rarely witnessed family conversations around feelings or dreams. So I naturally rationalized that limited sentimental communication must be normal for all couples. Having had no real previous role models for intimate connection and quality time, I further rationalized that Mr. CEO's spending so much time on his laptop instead of with me was also perfectly normal.

*He didn't come from a dysfunctional home like I did, so this must be normal, right?* is what I'd repeatedly think to myself. And my own internal critical message back to myself would be, *Just keep quiet and be grateful that someone from such a good home is willing to stay with you.* But deep down I was really sad that we rarely talked about anything of much significance other than Teddy. And it did bother me sometimes that when we took Teddy on those long, beautiful walks in the woods, our walks were often silent. But then I'd see the bright side that at least we could use the silence as an opportunity to watch Teddy explore, listen to the birds, and enjoy nature.

Eventually, I noticed the silence appeared to be associated with Mr. CEO being wrapped up in thought; meanwhile, conversations about those thoughts were off-limits. And speaking of our potential future was especially off-limits. I even resorted to calling marriage the "M word." When we did eventually get engaged after almost ten years of my wondering about our future, we still didn't discuss the future much. Finally, I noticed that I was feeling more needed than loved overall. But then again, at that time, I also thought feeling needed and feeling loved were one and the same, so I didn't give that awareness a second thought.

Inevitably, though, I craved more. I was starving for attention, affection, and communication. In almost desperate need of the same, I often acted dramatic and needy, very jealous, and very fearful of the many unknowns and uncertainties in our relationship. But the more I tried to get answers, the higher and more impenetrable the walls he put up to keep me out seemed to become. It was as if a line in the sand was drawn and I could get no closer. I spent years sitting on that line, watching and waiting for Mr. CEO to walk near it or to show signs that the walls might come down.

*All my focus was on him and very little of my focus was on me.*

Starving for approval and afraid of abandonment, I hung on to the crumbs metaphorically dropped onto the line for me. I'd scarf them up and wait for more, somehow believing I was lucky to have even that much. I was not noticing how easily bread-crumbs became a meal when starving was my new set point.

One of my closest friends routinely asked me, "Don't you want children? Isn't it time to tell him to shit or get off the pot?" And she was absolutely right in that I wanted to realize my vision of a home that included children. I wanted it all very much. However, ignoring my needs and abandoning myself had become such a way of life by then that her words bounced right off. I was spending my primary reproductive years running from the prospect of being left alone and jumping through hoops to gain approval, but I couldn't see what I was doing to myself.

I couldn't see even though the signs of self-harm were everywhere. I could see I was barely eating, but I blamed it on the absurd number of hours I was working to pay off my medical school loans. I could see Mr. CEO getting text messages on his phone, and then suddenly turn his phone facedown, putting the next incoming text message out of my view. At one point, while we were separately strolling through the aisles of Barnes & Noble, I turned a corner and found him talking to someone on his cell phone. As I approached, he quickly turned his back on me and walked out of earshot while I stood there, frozen.

That moment actually sent me into one of my first panic attacks, complete with a racing heart, chest tightness, and an immediate sense of connection to what my imagination told me that Mom may have been feeling in the kitchen on That Night in September when Dad was on the phone and waved her away. Dad could have been on the phone speaking to a family member, but since all I saw was that she was waved away while he was on the phone, and then within hours she was dead, my subconscious conclusion became that being waved away by your man while he is on the phone was an ominous sign.

It didn't help me believe anything different when my panic and suspicions were typically downplayed when I would ask about such calls. That dismissal of my reality quickly sent me to seek counseling on my own for thinking I was losing my mind. I definitely didn't trust Mr. CEO anymore, but worse than that, I no longer even trusted what I thought, knew, or saw.

*Staying out so late for work so many nights would be suspicious to anyone, right?*

*And what about that afternoon when he did a two-hour run in the pouring rain that turned into an eventual phone call asking me to please pick him up because his legs were too cramped to make it back?*

My insides screamed at me, accusing him of horrible things in my head, but I was still too distrustful of myself to believe anything I suspected. I instead rationalized, *No, I must be paranoid and/or going crazy. How could I think such thoughts about someone I say I love?* as well as many other self-shaming thoughts. Against my better judgment, I drove to pick him up. When I arrived, he was completely drenched from the rain. The only thing he said when he got into the car was "Sorry." Of course, he meant "sorry for inconveniencing you and making you drive over here in the rain." But following the spinning thoughts in my mind, I interpreted it as an apology for overall violating the essence of our commitment.

For me, that simple word *sorry* was my wake-up call. I had been previously convinced *sorry* was not part of his vocabulary. Prior to that day, I couldn't recall him ever using the word and had convinced myself it was because "perfect people" don't ever need to say sorry. This time, to finally hear him use the word snapped me out of my oblivion. Needless to say, a relationship without trust doesn't work well and we finally moved forward to making separation plans. But by then, I had no idea who I had become.

This was my life on autopilot: going through the motions as picture perfect and happy on the outside while living a sad, neglectful, wasted life behind closed doors. Except for my relationship with Teddy, not much in my life by that point had any real substance. Teddy had lived to be fourteen and a half, but he could no longer get up off of the floor without help due to lower spine and hip troubles. One day, while Mr. CEO was on a trip out of the country, Teddy died in my arms. My gratitude for having been part of Teddy's life, for the connection with him and experiencing the journey beside him, was very real. (Thank you, Theodore "Teddy" Bear. You were an angel to me.)

When Mr. CEO returned, we had a beautiful burial ceremony for Teddy. Possibly only because he may have wanted to honor our time with Teddy, Mr. CEO surprisingly agreed to my invitation to go to couples counseling so I could gain a sense of closure before we split. In my experience, it was rare to get closure and rare to get answers to unexplained questions when a relationship ends. No one had yet reached out to explain the background and details that led to my mother's death.

Once, I was searching Ancestry.com and stumbled on Mom and Dad's marriage certificate, which was dated ten months after I was born. I had already known that Dad wasn't at the hospital when I was born and I knew I was curiously born in the Midwest, even though we grew up in the Northeast. Yet, I had always just assumed they were married and living together at the time I was born. I also assumed that maybe Mom was visiting someone out West and she had given birth unexpectedly. I teased Dad incessantly for making me have to learn the details of my birth from an online source instead of directly from him. Providing answers and giving a sense of closure for my many unanswered questions about his relationship with Mom was not Dad's strong suit.

I had so many questions around the topic of relationships that getting closure with Mr. CEO felt promising for my personal growth. And, no surprise, therapy was absolutely rewarding for me. I was able to learn so much from that opportunity. My eyes were opened to so many of the relationship dynamics that I could see were pervasive in my past relationships and in my parents' relationship. I was fascinated and started to read about psychological concepts that were new to me, such as attachment theory, and I read books and articles by physician Dan Siegel, M.D., and psychologist Stan Tatkin, Psy.D., M.F.T., regarding its application to adult relationships.

I also dove into reading almost all of the books and articles on imago relationship therapy, a methodology co-created by psychologists Harville Hendricks, Ph.D., and Helen LaKelly Hunt, Ph.D. In their words, "our unconscious has its own agenda...to repair the damage done in childhood as a result of unmet needs, and the way it does that is to find a partner who can give us what our caretakers failed to provide."[1] In hindsight, it made perfect sense that I had been unknowingly hoping to get something from my previous partners that they would not consciously be able to give and that I didn't know how to give to myself.

I will save these fascinating relationship lessons for a different time and place, and only add here that discovering the many patterns of the human condition and our relationship dynamics proved to be both freeing and enlightening for me.

Therapy also helped me in the preparation for our ultimate separation, since ending anything after thirteen-plus years is never simple. I moved downstairs into the basement of the condo, and he stayed upstairs in the master bedroom on the second floor. The main floor, with its kitchen and combined dining/living room, was a common area where we passed each other as roommates. I still, however, needed to head to the second floor to use the closets and the main bathroom since it was the only bathroom with a shower.

One evening, Mr. CEO had gone back to his place of business to do more work; I was in the upstairs bathroom and noticed a new cologne in the cabinet. The cologne was called Gucci Guilty. Since I had never known him to wear cologne, or at least never to buy any, I guessed it must have been a gift. And even though everything was now out in the open, and I had already given back the engagement ring, and we were making concrete plans to go our separate ways, nothing could have prepared me for the floodgates of emotion that were opened in my heart by seeing that bottle of cologne.

My hands started to tremble and the room began to spin. I hunched over as I felt the most intense pain stabbing into my heart that I'd ever felt in my life. My gut felt like I'd vomit. I struggle even now to describe the sensations. My knees and legs weakened, and I could barely stay standing long enough to make my way back down the two flights of stairs to the basement. The pain seemed to be traveling up from a place deep and low inside of me.

Once I reached my bed in the basement, I lay down and wailed as if I were dying.

Upon seeing that cologne in the bathroom, I saw an image in my head of him huddled around the watercooler gossiping with colleagues. I pictured him laughing and mocking my life situation while he explained how someone other than me gifted him with a bottle of Gucci Guilty as a joke. I felt humiliated at the thought. This internal visual spiraled into a firm realization that I was literally here in a basement alone and lonely, and I had felt alone for most of my life.

These thoughts were compounded by others such as: *Not only have I been alone all my life, but the ones who were supposed to love me, supposed to care for me, supposed to have been in my corner and have my back did NOT have my back. It felt like they stabbed me in the back on top of it.*

In a state of despair, I could see that I was literally alone in the dark basement, a dungeon of my own making, which still smelled like my deceased dog. I knew of no one in my life whom I could call that I believed would be willing to be with me there in my moment of need. Meanwhile, the room kept getting darker as the night came. I had a sense that all of my bottled-up pain, anger, and confusion from That Night in September when I was alone in my bed as a child, That Night when Mom ended her own life, was the only thing coming to meet me there in that basement. And just like That Night, there would still be no one with me to explain why I was not worthy of someone willing to stay with me. No one there to answer why I was not worthy of even a parent's love. No one I could call would be able to answer that question for me—not my sister, not Dad, not my friends, not my colleagues.

The pain deepened to my very core and my cries were loud but reaching no one. There was a desperate grasping and reaching to feel someone, anyone, who could be there with me in that moment of need. Someone who could save me and take me away from feeling and seeing the painful truth of my life. That Night, as a child, I was not capable of feeling all of this. I instead needed to escape the reality that Mom had abandoned us, and I was able to escape it That Night by holding my dog and feeling nothing but emptiness. This time, however, there was no dog to cuddle, no longer a Teddy Bear to hold, and the feelings were inescapable.

*I was finally feeling it all with nowhere else to run, no identity to escape into.*

My protectors, who throughout my life were the Doctor, the Responsible One, the Workhorse, and the Obedient One, could no longer save me from facing my deep truth. The truth was, my life was one of abusing my body through sports in both high school and college in the name of getting approval and being obedient; of starving myself of food in the name of being too busy to eat; of starving myself of affection and living off the crumbs of an occasional hug or a nod in my direction in the name of feeling lucky someone would stay with me; of imprisoning myself in medical school and with credit card debt; of obligations and years of working myself to exhaustion in the name of desperately trying to prove and earn my worth; and, finally, of ungratefully pissing away my prime years of fertility in the name of a fear of abandonment.

*The truth was that I spent my life trying to prevent feeling this very pain, the pain that was born That Night I watched Mom turn her back on me and walk away from our lives forever.*

The pain of losing my mother birthed the belief that Mom turning her back and leaving me behind must have been justified because I had no worth and was nothing to her. I believed my very existence meant nothing. I believed that, in my father's eyes, my only worth was to be like the son he never had, hide who I was as a woman, and that love had to be earned. So I created all of those subconscious identities to be more acceptable to the world. From my little child's view, I deduced that who I was when I was authentically being myself, as opposed to one of those identities, was a child not even worthy of a mother's love. I had to be no more worthy than something you discard and walk away from.

*These were the explanations I subconsciously created at seven years old to make sense of my painful world and were the very beliefs that led me to a life of neglecting, abusing, and abandoning myself in return.*

That night in the basement, I cried in agony for hours until no tears were left. I started to wonder, *Was this also what Mom felt? Had she been begging to be removed from the truth of her life?*

*With that question, and as a glimpse of the slightest compassion for my mother's predicament entered my awareness, something else awakened in me to see that all of this is a choice.*

I could choose to escape into death as Mom did or I could choose to surrender to the truth of what my life had become and stop running. As painful, and even as pathetic as I thought my life had become, I chose to surrender to truth.

As I surrendered, I first allowed the feelings of my reality as a neglected, abandoned, and isolated soul to wash over me. Then, simultaneously, I could also feel my body start to relax. As I relaxed more and more and stopped resisting the facts I had been in denial about, there was a feeling of extreme relief that there was finally nowhere left to run. My chest relaxed, my breathing improved, and in pure exhaustion, I fell asleep.

As I drifted off, maybe in a dream, I heard what I can only describe as metallic, nonhuman-sounding voices nearby me having a conversation next to my bed while looking down at me. There was a distinct cadence to the words, and it repeated itself with the same cadence each time. I could only make out:

*With time, ba bop, ba bop, ba bop*
*With love, ba bop, ba bop, ba bop*
*With ?, ba bop, ba bop, ba bop*

The words weren't actually *ba bop,* but that is the best way I can think to describe the cadence of those words that I couldn't make out.

I also cannot say how many times those unclear words with a rhythmic cadence repeated themselves, maybe three or four times, before I realized I may be actually hearing something speaking and finally looked around the room to see who could be talking. My eyelids were swollen from crying and the room was pitch black, so without being able to see anything to explain what I heard, I just let out a big sigh of more surrender, rolled over, and went back to sleep.

When I awoke the next morning, I immediately remembered the night's events and felt a sense of calmness and peace. Something inside me knew, without question, that I had survived facing my deepest, most painful fears.

I also knew I had not been alone.

*Even a lace dress couldn't hide that I was hitting rock bottom.*

# PART TWO

*mothering the child inside*

CHAPTER 9

# *The Shift*

I used to leave movies or finish books feeling so unsatisfied and/ or annoyed, particularly if they were the kind of stories that took me on a deep dive into darkness and despair only to wrap up quickly with a nice happy bow. Like when, for at least 90 percent of the story, the "bad guys" got away with doing unspeakable things and then, right at the very end, there would there be a dramatic turn of events and the good guys prevailed and things suddenly worked out. This was upsetting to me because only giving me 5 percent, maybe 10 percent, tied in a happy bow and then only "the end" never felt like enough! It seemed so anticlimactic after all of the turmoil that the characters had gone through.

The movie *Taken* was one of those movies for me. Liam Neeson's character flies all over the world getting involved in unspeakable things and finally rescues his daughter from the slave trade just to get essentially a "Hey, thanks for bringing her home" from his ex-wife. What about giving us an amazing rise after the fall? What about giving us a satisfying taste of what a happily-ever-after can actually look like, instead of just a glimpse leaving us to never really see how mind-blowingly amazing life can be?!? Wouldn't celebrating in the light beyond the darkness make us all feel that much more victorious?!?

Well, here's to bringing on celebration! I fully intend on having you celebrate my victory! I want you to feel me rise like a phoenix from the ashes! Up until now, I've been giving you the details of my sorrows and woes and sometimes my just plain shitty attitude.

Speaking of my shortcomings, pardon me as I use this as a moment of thanks:

Thank you, Mr. CEO, for temporarily sharing your family with me. They helped fill a very deep void at the time and I am still very grateful. I'd like to believe I had a positive impact on them as well. I apologize to you for trying to take responsibility for what was yours and yours alone to own. Thank you for what I now consider a "sacred contract," as author and medical intuitive Caroline Myss might call it. My current belief is that my "contract" with you was to help me find my rock bottom, the exact place I needed to be to learn unconditional self-love.

But now I move on to share my experiences of triumph and beauty and reveal a glimpse into the feelings of the radiance of love and light after those dark days. I am truly appreciative of the brilliant gifts (gem lessons) I gained from my journey. Life has so much to love if we would only look!

CHAPTER 10

# Learning That Attention Matters

Wikipedia defines mindfulness as the "psychological process of bringing one's attention to experiences occurring in the present moment."[1]

*While still living on autopilot and not stopping long enough to notice,*

and before my rock bottom experience, there were actually a few important things I had already started to learn from living with Teddy that were starting to take root.

*One such lesson was that if I wanted a
change to happen, I had to make a change.*

My dream of having a home filled with true unconditional
love was still alive and well, and so in an attempt to prepare for
that dream, I made the decision that the first change needing to
happen was to sell my all-consuming medical practice.

I decided that taking a part-time position as an employee,
instead of continuing to be an owner of a private corporation,
would be the ideal next step. The rationale was that if I could at
least transfer the majority of the administrative responsibilities
to an employer, as well as cut back on the number of hours
I was spending at the office, then I could begin taking some
leisure time for myself. I knew my current overworking habits
typically created a sixty- to eighty-hour full-time workweek,
so I thought as a part-time employee, I could trick myself into
only actually working forty hours maximum. A forty-hour
workweek would make work feel like a vacation by comparison. While I entertained a couple of twenty-hours-per-week
part-time employee options working for hospital-owned medical practices, a third, albeit unusual but more compelling, opportunity surfaced that involved one of my mentors.

This mentor was a gifted potter, painter, and out-of-the-
box thinker who had become a successful specialist physician
and was sharing a different approach to delivering care to his
patients. He had already successfully built two offices with the

traditional medical model and then gone a step further when he added healing arts centers in adjacent spaces, complete with acupuncture, yoga, and other modalities. His third office was going to be his first integrated space, with the waiting room shelves full of books like *You Can Heal Your Body, The Power of Now, The Secret, The Alchemist,* and *The Four Agreements.*

He was creating a space where the healing arts practitioners and the medical staff would work alongside each other to support the patients and one another. As it turned out, this third office location was going to be in the same city where I was entertaining my other options. It also coincidentally turned out that he was looking to hire someone willing to work part-time while helping him oversee that third location's medical offerings and someone open to integrating these nontraditional offerings with the usual medical treatments.

The combination of being a part-time employee and working in an environment that was much more conducive to the new life I was hoping to create seemed too good to be true. We knew I could bring so much more to the position than he had bargained for and that this would be a true win-win for both of us. So, with nothing more than a handshake, we embarked on a venture that would prove mutually beneficial in so many ways, and gained a close friendship to boot.

Another coincidence occurred when I approached my lawyer about the early termination of the lease for my medical office. My lawyer simply smiled at me as he delivered the news and said, "Your landlord happens to be my client, too. I know he'll be happy to let you out of your lease early and without penalty since he's been eyeballing that space for his plans to expand."

Finally, if these weren't enough signs that this opportunity was an open door with my name on it, as I moved forward with making plans for the move, I realized in my excitement I had forgotten to ask for the address of this new third office before agreeing to work in it. It could have easily been way across the city, but I really hadn't cared how far the commute would be since this venture felt like the perfect change I needed. Happily, it was only a six-minute drive away from the condo where I'd be living.

This beautiful new office was located in a gutted old mansion in a historic section of the city with a spa atmosphere and a Pottery Barn—furnished waiting room with a fireplace and mantel. We had cucumber water for guests, French doors into our examining room area, an upstairs yoga studio, spa showers with multiple jets, massage rooms, and at least three outdoor spaces to lounge. Most patients were confused and wondered *had they really walked into a medical doctor's office? Did they get the address wrong?*

I recall the staff from his primary and founding office had actually been resistant to his introduction of these new healing arts ideas; some were even angered by my mentor's requirement for us to say "My pleasure" in response to a patient's "Thank you." Change can be challenging. But for me, all of these small touches and extra thoughtfulness that had not, in my experience, ever been considered in the world of medicine made coming to work an absolute pleasure. My work hours had been cut to a third of what they had been for so many years, and I had taken time back to get a full night's sleep, to get one-on-one Pilates training to strengthen my core (literally and figuratively), and to get back the quality time that I desired. This was all coming together with just deciding to make a change in the direction of my dreams.

I also remember some of my employer's longtime staff giving him a really hard time at first about making the changes because "real doctors don't talk about healing or spirituality or meditation." In an effort to convince the skeptics that he had not lost his mind, he gave us all iPods loaded with the audiobooks of the same books on the shelves and asked us to listen to see he wasn't making up these ideas. In a mandatory all-hands meeting, he told us that there were many practices that have been around for years which could potentially help our patients, and he encouraged us to have an open mind.

I took the little red iPod he gave me and listened to it while exercising and during my commute to the office. Much of what I was listening to resonated with me and I wanted more. I was so intrigued by these ideas, brand-new to me, but also so familiar. They seemed to have the same essence of the God I knew as a child and the same essence of what I wanted people to experience when they visited me in my dream home. So I devoured those books with a hunger I had not known I had. Each book introduced me to a new author, and I would then search for other works by that author to take me to deeper levels with the concepts they were feeding me.

The first author to teach me to direct my focus and attention inward instead of grasping outward was Eckhart Tolle. I first listened to *The Power of Now,* then to his other books about "the now," "stillness," and "presence" as a means to connecting to the "oneness" of everything. I especially enjoyed listening to his recorded retreats on the same topics and to hear him personally tell his story of moving from deep depression and suicidal thoughts to the joy he found in the simple act of presence. I'm very likely not giving his message the proper depth of delivery, but he was my first "signpost," as he might say.

In *The Power of Now,* Tolle refers to something he calls the *pain body,* and he offers an exercise wherein instead of running from your pain you become present and witness it. I was introduced to this exercise during the time period shortly after that rock-bottom night in the condo basement. Feeling the breakup and learning the truth of what had been my existence so far, especially thinking about the wasted years and neglected needs, still involved significant pain. I had been trying to live one day at a time, but often found myself overwhelmed with the raw, fresh wound of being separated from my chosen partner, even if that partnership had not been healthy. So, from a place of nothing to lose, I gave this new practice a try.

I got into comfortable clothes and laid still on my bed, breathing slowly and deeply. I could sense my brain and thoughts were continually leaving the room to run down the rabbit hole of stories surrounding the cause of this pain. But once I was able to notice this outward-focused, I was then able to refocus my mind inwardly. With eyes closed, I intentionally searched for the origin from which this raw pain could be emanating. And then, to my surprise, I found it, right in the middle of my chest and extending out and toward the left, within the space where my physical heart was as well.

I kept my attention there in the center of my chest and said something to myself like, *Ahhh, I see you now. I don't know or have a clue how to fix this yet, but I'm here with you now.*

And that very moment, the pain transformed to a warm, soothing heat that spread across my chest into my back and upward to my throat. It was awesome. I was afraid it would end as quickly as it arrived, but I didn't want it to end.

If you've ever used and icy-hot ointment or hot wet-packs layered on sore aching muscles and felt the resulting relaxation, then you know the feeling; this was similar to that, but the sensation came from deeper on the inside. I basked in the warmth of what I imagined was pain melting away, and I drifted off to sleep. In the morning, there only remained a dull ache, but the previous intense piercing rawness had dissipated for that time. This new idea of looking inward was proving to be an amazing first step home to myself.

*I was experiencing positive growth opportunities simply from intentionally placing myself in an environment that was aligned with who I wanted to become.*

Many new ideas and growth opportunities continued to arise from the content on that little red iPod. Our healing arts center began offering vision board workshops where I was able to learn another method of focusing my attention on what I wanted instead of on what I didn't want, but this time through a collage of images instead. I used my vision board as a reminder of my desires and to play with another concept new to me, that of the Law of Attraction. Since there is so much already out there that is worth reading, let me leave it here for now that the Law of Attraction essentially says that like attracts like; or our world at any moment is a reflection of our own focused energy.

And yet another author from the iPod collection, Louise Hay, taught me to use affirmations connected to the vision on my vision board as an additional, reinforcing layer of focus. Hay's work is filled with thought-provoking positive affirmations, such as, "Life supports me in every possible way," or "I live in the paradise of my own creation."[2] I listened to every audiobook from her that I could get my hands on. It was now clear to me that, up until that time in my life, my attention had rarely been focused on appreciation for the positive aspects of my life (except with Teddy) and so I was eager to make this change.

I decided to put into practice what I was learning from Louise Hay while searching for a new home. I first visualized what kind of house would feel really good to come home to after work. I was enjoying my position at the combined medical and healing arts center and I was willing to commute if need be. I imagined an ideal home environment would be one most conducive for picking up the pieces of my broken heart while also instilling me with optimism about creating a new life. I quickly realized that a newer, beautiful, low-maintenance apartment was ideal. I pictured wood floors, granite countertops, and a spectacular view.

*Ahhh, perfect!* Once that was clear, I then immediately knew exactly where I could get a great view!

The clear choice was to move to one of the nearby Finger Lake towns where my girlfriends and I would periodically go for a getaway at a famous luxury French-inspired inn and spa. The primary associations for me with that town were of those relaxing spa days, its gorgeous lake views, nearby wine tasting opportunities, and my favorite Italian restaurant to top it off. During the winter there, in preparation for the holidays, the town looked like it was the backdrop of a Hallmark Movie with gingerbread-inspired houses, a gazebo in front of the lake's pier, Christmas carolers in full costume on the corner, and horse-drawn carriages for tourists. Yes, this town would be perfect. If any place said, "Come here to heal," it was there.

As I scheduled my apartment viewings, I repeatedly recited my favorite Louise Hay-inspired affirmations.

- ◆ "I only live in beautiful, amazing spaces."
- ◆ "My perfect home is being prepared for me. If I haven't found it yet, it's just because it's still being prepared."

I optimistically set out on weekend trips to the lake to find this new home. I made three trips in total, with multiple apartment viewings, but none of the spaces felt like they fit what I was visualizing for myself. As the realtor and I left the last property option on her list, she apologized with discouragement in her voice when I told her, "No, none of these will work for me." And with our heads hanging down in defeat as we walked back to our cars, the realtor proclaimed, "Wait! I've got it!"

She then explained that she'd forgotten there was a historic brick building right across the street from the lake. There were retail shops and restaurants on the street level, but the upper floors had been converted into individual condos for purchase. They had been in the approximate price range of $300,000–$800,000, depending on each's view and number of bedrooms. But it turned out that the owner had held out for too long waiting for people willing to pay the higher price on several of the units; as a result, the property almost went into foreclosure. Next, local investors decided to capitalize on this opportunity, and they were literally still in the process of turning these condos into rental units.

*Coincidentally*, they would be available for rent starting as early as one month from that day. They technically weren't even posted as being available for rent yet, so that's why they hadn't crossed her mind.

The realtor quickly checked her office for a set of keys and we ran up the stairs to view a couple of condos that were within my budget. They were exactly what I had been looking for! As one of the first people to view them, I had the privilege to choose from multiple units. I chose a cozy one-bedroom with a den that could serve as a second bedroom for guests when it was closed off with its pocket doors. The unit also had two bathrooms (one with a bath/shower and the other off of the bedroom with another shower). It had ceiling-to-floor windows in all the rooms overlooking Main Street, and its view of both the lake and the gazebo was ideal.

The inside of the building was newly remodeled, while the outside was beautifully old, historic, and brick. I was going to be able to have my granite countertops, my hardwood floors, my stainless-steel fixtures, and my low-maintenance perfect apartment by the lake that I had envisioned after all, and I would be only paying a small monthly rent compared to the $399,000-plus someone else would have had to pay to own it! I chose to believe this was just like the affirmation said: "I hadn't found it prior because it was still being prepared for me."

To this day, I still love house-hunting and will offer to do it for friends. I fully believe it's now only a matter of shifting my attention and choosing only to live in beautiful spaces with gorgeous views. Since this shift in attitude, my choices have given me a gorgeous view of pristine Skaneateles Lake, an amazing high-rise southeast view of San Francisco and the Bay, and, as I write this book, I am looking out of the window at a "Pinch me, we're right on the water" view of the Hudson River in Westchester County.

## Disidentification from the Obedient One

Perhaps the biggest step toward having what I wanted and needed was the to look inward and make choices by asking, "What do I really want and what do I need?" My usual way previously had been to look outward for approval or for other people to tell me what I should want or was allowed to have. I would jump through their hoops and follow their rules, hoping to prevent danger and earn approval, or thinking it would secure their love and attention. But this new practice of looking inward to discern my needs and wants proved that the answers were already right there and I could make my own rules.

These were freeing, invigorating concepts. *Create my own rules? Co-create my own life? What?! Wow!*

The beauty of rock bottom is that there is nothing to lose. Given this fact, I embraced these new concepts and tried them on for size. And the Obedient One identity happily put down her rulebook and allowed me to take the lead.

# CHAPTER 11

# Life by the Lake: My Safe Transformation Cocoon

Living lakeside was everything I dreamed it would be. In the mornings, on my commute to the combined healing arts center, I was in awe of how gorgeous the lake was at 6 AM. The water was so still and sparkling that often I would pull over to take a photo. This was before Instagram, so the photo was just a chance to capture the moment simply for myself. The sunsets on my commute home were equally surreal.

I decorated the apartment with whatever made me happy, including a very high bed to jump into like a princess, a custom upholstered settee that I envisioned going into my home office one day, and three splendid oriental rugs with colors that perfectly tied in to the feel of each room. During the holidays, the carolers below serenaded me from the corner, and I spent many,

many more spa days hanging out with my girlfriends. Pampering myself in such a way had been missing for far too long.

## Disidentification from the Workhorse

I also used the new "what do I want?" approach to choose my exercise regimen. The old no-pain/no-gain, push-your-body-to-test-your limits model was far from my cup of tea. The thought of going to an actual gym felt like I'd be dragging the Workhorse out of the green, open pastures where she now happily romped and pulling out the riding crop to whip her toward some arbitrary "betterment" of herself. Even the words used by most athletic trainers and coaches at the time still triggered me with the almost sadomasochistic punishment ring to them. Phrases like *Whip you into shape, Kick your own ass,* or *Feel the burn that hurts so good* were the opposite of inspiring. For me, those phrases created a reaction similar to an abused dog flinching when someone nearby unknowingly lifts their hand quickly to point at something.

At least one perk to all the years of intense exercise I'd put in—I still had very little body fat to speak of, a very high metabolism, and a muscular body type that was appealing to men. The perks of a long history of intense workouts and competition made being able to wear any clothes I desired an easy and normal way of life.

*But as I applied the new inward-looking techniques I'd been learning, my body revealed multiple hidden painful and/or numb areas that still desperately needed my attention.*

The tendons around my ankles, now seemingly barely holding my feet to my lower legs, reminded me that when I no longer experienced pain and swelling, even if I severely twisted my ankle, it was not a good thing, but a sign of years of neglect.

My legs, riddled with scar tissue and damaged fascia from repetitive and countless torn ligaments, muscle sprains, and tears, reminded me of years of self-abuse instead of appreciation.

My hips, with now almost rigid inflexibility, reminded me of many times I had been in mid-competition and in excruciating pain, and how, instead of giving myself attention and care, I had allowed the athletic trainers to tape my hips to my thighs to the point of numbness so I could still run in the finals.

Finally, the mirror itself, which doesn't lie, reminded me that if my ribs were showing on my chest this meant I had not eaten well enough for the last two years due to being overly consumed with "what he might be up to now" and culminating in the lonely emptiness of living out of a basement.

Although there were negative associations with exercise, I still knew there were real benefits to be had from regular exercise. So, I visualized what exercise could look like for me in the new life I was creating. From asking this question, I discovered I only really wanted to exercise for the benefits of how good it felt to move my body and for the positive impact on my health. I found that incorporating walking around the lake created new positive associations since being out in nature and being near water was somehow both soothing and invigorating. Walking also reminded me of the long, fun walks I had taken with my beloved Teddy.

Finally, I found I really wanted to do an exercise that would strengthen my core. While still only a couple of months out from that rock-bottom night in the basement and still nursing my wounds, I knew that although my body appeared to be outwardly strong, my core, both literally and figuratively, was not. So, for this intention, I chose a private Pilates instructor to help me solidly rebuild my strength from the inside out. This Pilates studio coincidentally turned out to be only a block's walk away from my lakeview apartment. Those sessions fit perfectly with the new life I was creating by the lake.

Meanwhile, the Workhorse trotted away and retired to play in the pastures now that I had unbridled her, removed her saddle, and hung up the riding crop.

## Disidentification from the Responsible One

Life by the lake was proving to be exactly what I needed. As I gazed outside from my settee to view the gorgeous lake one weekend, I realized I had indeed created the perfect, safe, transformational, cocoon-like environment. I then further realized this was the very first time in my life since the age of seven that I hadn't felt obligated to be responsible for anyone except myself. Dad was doing fine; he had many girlfriends taking care of him. My sister was immersed in her life with her husband and their son. There was no longer a dog or a boyfriend for me to attend to, and changing from being an employer to an employee meant I was no longer required to dedicate nearly as many hours or sacrifice as much time to doing paperwork as I had done in my previous medical career positions.

*I was free to make my own decisions and
I could put myself as a priority.*

I realized I could finally play with imagining whatever future that seemed the most appealing to me and then made an agreement with myself to take whatever steps made sense to me (even if only to me) that would propel me toward my desired future. And with that, the Responsible One sang hallelujah and took a long overdue, restorative nap.

So, what did I want my future to look like?

One potential version of the future was to remain by the lake. I had a job I loved and a perfect apartment. I had my girlfriends who loved to visit me, especially since there was the added perk of the local luxury spa. My sister especially enjoyed visiting me during the holidays since living in the South for her meant missing out on a white Christmas with snow, decorated gingerbread-like houses, and bright lights lining the streets. On one Christmas visit, she made us go out into the bitter cold to take photos and create a Hallmark movie–worthy scene with her and her husband in the gazebo by the lake. I was confident when I visualized this version of my potential future that I would be perfectly happy, safe, and comfortable. I also had no doubts that it would be conducive to easily creating my dream home life there in that quaint lake town.

However, in addition to my dream home, there were now many new and untapped dreams waiting for me that I had only just begun to explore. And although this new vision of an alternative potential future was still foggy, what was clear was that I no longer wanted to unconsciously repeat patterns and reinforce identities/narratives that no longer served me. I knew I was now signed up for more than just being safe and comfortable.

*I wanted to keep unlearning the patterns of self-abandonment and neglect that I had mastered, and I wanted to continue learning more and more about co-creating with Spirit/ God/Source/the Universe and thriving in a beautiful new life without fear.*

So, I dove even deeper into this new life education by absorbing as many books, workshops, speeches, and resources as were available to me. I focused on the subjects of purposeful or intentional living, visioning, and mindfulness, and on looking inward for my answers. I wanted to learn all that I possibly could for my own personal growth and healing, and for whatever future untold benefits were in store. I wanted to learn how to apply all of this amazing education to my own relationship patterns and to be better prepared for my potential future partner and family. While at work in the integrated center, I made sure to expose myself to all of the new modalities and practices made available to us, including acupuncture, yoga, maya massage, and reiki—anything to further my fascinating life education.

Yes, for sure, this cocoon by the lake I'd set up provided the perfect space for my transformation. Thank you, Eckhart Tolle, Michael A. Singer, Reverend Michael Bernard Beckwith, Dr. Daniel J. Siegel, Byron Katie, Don Miguel Ruiz, James Allen, Howard Thurman, Dr. Wayne Dyer, Shakti Gawain, Louise Hay, Carolyn Myss, and Dr. Harville Hendrix, and Alison A. Armstrong for being there by the lake with me. Thank you, Oprah Winfrey, as well. Through your interviews, you gave me closer glimpses of these and many other amazing life educators. You were ALL beautiful angels to me.

One amazing healing example of applying the wisdom I was gaining from these life educators was when I applied a combination of newly learned tools to help further soothe and heal my still raw and aching heart. Most days I was mindful of a constant mild soreness in the center of my chest. This ache reminded me to be ginger and compassionate with myself as I was still on the mend. But on occasion, I would attach myself to a thought of my painful childhood or to a thought of how I very likely may never be able to trust a man again, and then, just as if I had reopened a wound, that sore ache would change to an intense, agonizing pain. Each time that happened, I would wonder if my heart would ever heal.

On one unforgettable weekend afternoon by the lake, I decided to try a combination of practices I had been learning. I chose the practices that were intended to help me stop running away from my pain, and instead looked inwardly toward it. The focus was on learning how to compassionately be with it and give it my full attention. So, with this as my intention, I looked inward at the place from which the pain seemed to be emanating and I repeated to myself, *I see you, I'm here.*

I then began to visualize what might be energetically happening on the inside. I could feel what I can only describe as an anxious, outwardly grasping sensation, like tentacles searching again for something to touch, something to be connected to. I visualized these heart tentacles with raw, oozing edges from where they had once been connected to someone, but then abruptly torn away.

This image of my heart in distress inspired me to ask myself this question: *What can I do to possibly help my heart's "tentacles" feel less sore and stop them from needing to desperately reach out for something that I know they won't find right now?*

Immediately, the answer came in the form of an image of a warm moat filled with sparkly pink, viscous fluid surrounding my heart. I visualized gently guiding each raw tentacle's end back inward toward the heart itself and down into the soothing, healing fluid of the surrounding moat. As each raw end submerged into this warm, thick fluid, the entire area felt more relaxed and comforted. I kept my focus on the imagined feeling of being able to gift my heart this imaginary healing bath.

Then, there it was again. That warm, melting sensation I'd had when I first practiced the inward-looking exercise from Eckhart Tolle in the condo's basement. I had now come to expect and love that feeling that I later dubbed the Alchemy of Melting Cares, and with it, any remnant of residual intensely anxious, grasping energy dissipated.

*It was another amazing reinforcement of my
own ability to give loving attention to myself.*

Equipped with these new, very effective tools, I was gaining confidence that I was fully capable of meeting my own needs and of moving through even the most traumatic of pain. And while fervently devouring all the nourishment that I could from the aforementioned abundance of resources, I stumbled onto a listing for a retreat intended for "Women of Elevated Worth." Since this was aligned with the vision of what I wanted for myself, I quickly signed up. It felt like yet another perfectly timed coincidence.

Finally, I had also started to notice members of the opposite sex again. The exact moment of awareness that this part of me was finally feeling better was at the pickup window in the pharmacy. I remember noticing how attractive the pharmacist was. Then I noticed that I had actually stopped listening to what he was saying altogether and was instead admiring his wavy hair, his smiling eyes, his rugged jaw, and his full lips. I giggled all the way home and celebrated that I was healing and getting closer to being ready to explore the romantic part of my life again!

My new approach of fully showing up in my daily life also included intentionally choosing to flirt when I felt like it, allowing myself to smile more, and deciding that I would focus on Eckhart Tolle's advice of being present in the *now.* And even though I still hadn't gained enough weight yet to be sufficiently healthy, with this new approach I was radiating the more attractive energy of curiosity. I was so much happier focusing on the moment and on this amazing life. My new approach to life was also in stark contrast to what I had been accustomed to doing; specifically, always having an expectation of what I believed each moment should be like. Dropping expectations and just being present opened the door wide to being pleasantly surprised by life.

In preparation for the retreat, the host encouraged participants to put into practice many similar ideas to those I was already practicing, so I suspected the retreat would be a good stepping-stone for me. I also decided to make a list for myself of the characteristics I was looking for in an ideal partner and I placed my focus on actually being those things myself that I was hoping for in someone else. For instance, if my list said I wanted a man to be "someone inspirational," I would next look inward at what ways I could be more of an inspiration myself. I was testing the theory that I attract the same energy that I put out.

Well, all of this new energy and pep in my step apparently also grabbed the attention of an acquaintance at the integrated office. He was also employed by the founder of the integrated center. He had been part of the contracting company that renovated our old historic office space and converted it into the soothing combined healing arts space it had become. Our employer ultimately entrusted him to help open up a healing arts café in our location as well.

I admit that I, too, found this acquaintance of the male "persuasion" fascinating, being especially fond of how much he oozed creativity. At our employer's request, his personal paintings decorated the walls of the integrated center, and our clients would randomly ask to pay him to buy a painting although the pieces were never officially for sale. I also appreciated how he was committed to challenging himself and learning everything he could with any resource at his disposal. Finally, and coincidentally, he, too, had been hiding away in a basement, since that is where the café in our building was located.

I absolutely knew bigger and better things were in store for him, so I finally asked him, "What in the world are you doing down here in this basement café when you have so many talents?!?" He must have been excited that I had seen him for who he really was, so he decided to confide in me that during his off hours he was actually working on an alternative plan for his future. It turned out that his friends, who already worked in Silicon Valley, saw how his wheat-pasting street art required advanced technical knowledge of Photoshop and they had encouraged him to apply for a graphic arts position out in California near them. For me, it was fun and inspiring to hear about his plans; unknown to us, we were coincidentally in parallel and complementary stages of our lives.

You've probably guessed this, but we did find ourselves dating. As we had learned we had very similar taste in music, our first date was at a local jazz festival. This man was one of the few people I had met in my adult life who was familiar with the music I grew up hearing as a child. He actually had "old school" albums on his playlist. And that date is still one of the top ten moments in my life so far. We walked around the jazz festival grounds listening to the different musicians, effortlessly talking, eating, and appreciating the evening.

As the sun was setting, we stumbled upon a bean bag lounging area and he asked if I'd like to have a seat. While seated, he eventually leaned back, and with an arm raised behind me, he invited me to lean in. I lay back, and to my pleasant surprise, I fit perfectly under his raised arm. My body felt that usual tingle of excitement that comes with the first touch of a new romantic interest, but simultaneously I also experienced a full-body relaxation that I can only describe as my body telling me, *This is what "home" feels like.* This brand-new combination of intense excitement and full-body relaxation was so unfamiliar that it was almost too much to process emotionally. So, I immediately jumped up and sat upright again in complete shock. He, in turn, teased me and said, "Fail," having no idea why I pulled away so abruptly.

Later in the evening, when the stars were now in the sky and the music was still filling the night air, we decided to head back to the bean bag lounge area. This time, I snuggled into position under his arm and we lay there looking up at the stars and enjoyed the moment. Then, when it couldn't get more perfect for a first date, a line of ten-plus tourists with cameras walked over to us. An elderly gentleman with a cane was leading the group and he stopped right in front of us and said something in their native language to the rest of the group. Meanwhile, I whispered to my creative date, "What is going on?"

He simply replied, "Shhh, enjoy the moment."

The tourist leader then stepped aside, and one by one, as they looked down at us on the bean bag, the group took our picture. I imagined they could see what I was feeling. It still makes me smile to think that somewhere out there, probably across the ocean, there are photos of us on those bean bags.

To everyone's surprise except mine, this creative contract worker/barista-by-day, artist-by-night went on to get the position as a production designer for a globally prestigious company in Silicon Valley. His departure was certainly bittersweet, but I knew I would be forever grateful for those moments with him when I practiced showing up and being fully present in a relationship without trying to be someone whose identity wasn't really mine. This would also be my first relationship without any trace of grasping to stay connected from a fear of abandonment.

When he left, I was so happy to have felt what relationship could be like when I focused on being present in each moment and not on distracting expectations. Having said that, it was not all completely roses. It would have been naive of me to think I was suddenly skilled at relationship or at being alone. But I knew I was still learning, so I gave myself compassion when I intermittently found myself struggling with missing my creative friend a bit too much. The grasping energy would return at times, but I was able to pay attention; notice. And I noticed that feeling always seemed to return when I was attached to or overly identified with a thought of abandonment such as, *What if I never get to experience anything like that again??*

Ultimately, with further practice in looking inward, and after going on some not-so-interesting dates just because I thought I should, as well as due to my connections to a few very supportive girlfriends, I could eventually and officially say I let my creative friend go to live his new amazing life in California. Meanwhile, I continued to commit myself to focus on the upcoming women's retreat as the next step in creating my own new amazing life.

# CHAPTER 12

# *Reunited with Lou*

The retreat was at a hotel resort on a beautiful beachfront. While there, I was thankful to be able to meet some amazing and inspiring women from around the globe. Just getting away for the sole reason of investing in myself was a perfect way to reinforce what I had already been learning on my own. There were multiple opportunities to further assess what was most important to me and why, and then to come up with practical action steps for implementing change in that direction. But why I am most grateful for having decided to attend that retreat is due to what happened after the retreat had ended. The retreat became a catalyst to awaken my desire to reunite with Lou.

After the retreat ended, I tried to visualize what it might be like if I were young again with this opportunity just to be there on the beach. As I walked along the edge of the water practicing stillness, instead of turning my focus inward on any painful or uncomfortable area, I visualized having a conversation with that little one of my youth. I wanted to imagine what it would be like if she were really right there with me on the beach.

What would she want to say, or want to do, or want me to hear?

As I looked out on the tide and at the birds flying by, I imagined her, a sweet younger version of me, walking along the side of me, kicking up sand with her steps. I asked her what she wanted to do, and I pictured her look up at me, giggle, and run toward the waves then back to me. The biggest awareness that came to me with this visualization was that she just wanted permission to play.

*She just wanted permission to play.*

She didn't tell me this in words; instead, I could imagine a look in her eye and the associated feeling, and then I could picture her running, spinning, splashing in the waves, and chasing the birds. Another part of me felt very maternal and my heart swelled up with joy. Tears flowing, I felt like my insides were smiling at the pure joy of feeling free to play and to just be there with myself on the beach.

As I watched Lou run toward the birds, then back to me, or splash in the waves while intermittently looking back at me, I had the realization of what she/I had missed in our youth and still very much needed. We wanted that feeling of being free. Free not only to play but also to explore the world around us while still feeling confident that someone was there to run back to should we need them. We were missing that feeling of a parent on a park bench at the playground that allows a child to feel safe to explore all the while with the knowing feeling that the parent is right behind them. At this moment on the beach, I was being my own parent, and for the first time that I could remember, Lou and I felt safe to play in this world.

That feeling that I could go play with confidence because I had my own back was indescribable. My body completely relaxed and there was nowhere else I wanted to be, except there with me on the beach. There was no energy in me grasping for anyone else to have to be there with us. There were no distracting thoughts of "shoulds" or responsibilities. No pull of my thoughts toward the past or the future. We were perfectly happy and fulfilled to be there together without focusing on anything except that moment. There was just a spacious open beach, a spacious open sky, and a spacious open heart with my little girl feeling free to fly like the birds.

# PART THREE

## majestic child

# CHAPTER 13

# *Free to Follow My Heart*

After the retreat I returned to the combined healing arts center energized by prioritizing time for myself and giving my little one the freedom to play. It was exciting that I had followed through. I wondered how many other ways Lou hoped to play that I hadn't yet allowed. The area that came to mind was relationships. Although I had allowed my creative friend to see more of me than anyone else ever had, I knew I had not completely let Lou out to play. In my previous long-term relationships, I usually was super serious, and had a lot of expectations for how a partner should or shouldn't behave. But when I looked inside myself, I found that, most of all, I really wanted my relationships be fun.

This immediately led me to make another list of the things I had wanted in a future partnership, which included, but were not limited to:

- Feeling safe enough in my partner's presence to bring out my little one so we can play together. He, too, needed to be in touch with his inner child.

- Sharing compatible values and priorities. (Wouldn't that be an amazing first?!)

- Being with someone open to new experiences and adventures. (For years I had deprived myself of exploration to learn which things excited me.)

- Wanting the same mind-blowing "home" feeling I'd had when I was seated with my creative friend on the bean bags during our first date.

- Being with someone who saw the real me, even at my "worst," and still loved what he saw.

- Having an equal passion for growth and expansion, even if it is uncomfortable.

- Someone who brings out the fullest authentic expression of me in their presence and who is my cheerleader so I can become even more than I think I can be. And I wanted to do the same for him.

- Spending regular, consistent, quality time together (especially as I was finally learning how precious it is to give that kind of attention to myself).

- Someone to travel with, sing and dance with, and be creative with.

- Sharing the same awe for nature and animals, and, of course, Spirit/God/Source/the Universe.

You can imagine this list quickly became lengthy. But it was so fun and inspiring to think that if I could get clear on what I wanted it would actually be possible.

I also began to get clearer on what I would want my future to look like in the area of my career. When it really came down to it, I liked the idea of making a positive impact on people's lives that medicine allowed, but I realized I'd prefer to be using the skills I enjoyed AND was good at; not only doing what I was good at. For instance, yes, I had talent on the track field, primarily due to inheriting Dad's genes and buttloads of training, but if I had also looked at my choice from a place of "What do I enjoy?" then I likely would have: A) chosen to invest in my intelligence by sticking only with the academic scholarship to college since I value growth and learning; B) chosen something like dance as a means to move my body and stay healthy (referring back to that gymnastics coach who saw something in me on the dance floor), instead of running and working out in a gym; and C) chosen also to sign up for music classes to fill more of my things-I-enjoy cup.

Yes, I had a brain that could process science and medicine, but I knew I would not have chosen the medical field for my career had I asked the question:

*What do I enjoy doing almost tirelessly*
*because the work inspires me at my core?*

Believing better late than never, I asked myself, *What was it exactly in the current medical position that inspires me at my core?* and the answers came surprisingly quickly. I could start to see with clarity that it wasn't as much the medicine, but the spiritual and healing components that my employer, the founder of the healing arts center, had allowed to be integrated into my work. I enjoyed creating a soothing spa-like atmosphere, created with attention to beauty and detail, like an inviting home. I enjoyed the expansive ideas coming from the books on the shelves in the waiting room and the little iPod in my pocket. I enjoyed the energy of being in an environment that welcomed alternative forms of healing like yoga and Reiki. Finally, I enjoyed the overall focus on the positive intention that remained a common thread among the support staff that I had personally hand-selected from the applicants when we opened.

I was also inspired by the patients that came to the combined healing arts center because they, like us, were desirous of experiencing a different paradigm, especially in the delivery of medicine. As one client expressed to me through tears when I casually mentioned to her that on the ultrasound image her ovaries looked "beautiful," this was "the first time in years she didn't feel like the physician was reminding her of how broken she is." This sentiment spoke volumes for me and it was what I wanted to carry forward into the future.

In the medical world I had previously known, care providers focused ever so much on the problems that I could easily see how a patient could believe they were broken. Then, from that view of brokenness, there's not much room to tap into those beautiful perfectly functioning aspects of themselves as a means to assist them in the healing of their whole being.

Patients at the combined healing arts center had started asking to book time with me, even if just on the phone, to help them see something positive in their situation despite whatever ailment they were facing. The time I spent with patients and staff alike shifted from conversations about medicine to focusing on how to move forward positively when they were feeling scared or broken. Many believed they were doomed to a miserable future, but it was usually because they were focusing on one shitty situation or another. They longed to be able to see a future filled with possibilities.

*Together we were learning that perspective matters. Shifting perspective allows us to see more possibilities and previously hidden opportunities.*

Some people came to me asking how they could muster the inner strength to move forward, such as the patient who was stuck between: A) wanting to make another attempt at having the baby she desperately wanted, and B) giving up and running away in fear because she'd already had twelve miscarriages.

Others came burdened with their what-ifs. They might ask:

♦ "What if I can't lose the weight and my diabetes gets the best of me?"

♦ "What if I am too old and I can never have a biological baby of my own?"

- "What if my partner doesn't love me anymore because of this horrible diagnosis since this is not what they signed up for?"

But the answer that seemed to lead to the most powerful shift in perspective was if I replied, "OK, what if?"

I wouldn't leave them with that, of course. I'd figuratively and sometimes literally hold their hands as they played out their personal narratives of a terrifying potential what-if future. I would make sure to never "let go of their hand," so to speak, until they could also imaginatively walk down at least three other possible future roads. As they allowed themselves to open up their minds and creatively envision how several futures could look, they almost inevitably could then positively move forward and face what previously had kept them stuck.

Even if they were just able to move to the inner place where they could somehow see themselves living with that worst-case scenario and still being OK with it, well, that was relief enough. But usually, walking through that first door of relief would then lead them to the next door of possibility, and then the next door, until they could decide which door felt best for them to choose. And often, realizing they could choose which door to go through added a layer of excitement when they moved in that direction.

*At the heart of it all, the perspective*
*was always what mattered.*

Later on, I would learn that helping someone attain a broader perspective and gain awareness is a *core competency* of professional coaching. I had already been putting this skill into practice.

In addition to the patients, I was also assisting members of our staff in having breakthroughs of their own. I started replacing the usual performance reviews with what I called *vision meetings*. For example, one of our front desk employees was making multiple errors and getting increasingly discouraged about her job, to the point where it was often obvious to the patients she greeted that she was uncomfortable. In her next vision meeting, she explained that she was feeling stuck because she didn't see any growth potential in the front desk position; her real love was using her hands-on skills.

It turned out that this woman had only taken the front desk position due to an injury that required her to step back from doing what she loved. But her injury had long since healed, and because working at the front desk paid the bills, she had settled for squeezing in a couple of clients on her days off.

Together, we walked further down the path of this one discouraging future she had locked herself into, and we could see that on this trajectory she would either remain miserable or potentially lose her job due to making constant mistakes. She could also quickly see that those mistakes were actually only due to distracting herself with thoughts of how much she wasn't enjoying the front desk job.

We then brainstormed alternate visions for her future, with small, buildable steps in them. We quickly landed on asking "What if you could flip your own formula?" For example, instead of working most hours at the front desk and doing only a few hours of hands-on services, she could spend the majority of her time doing the work she loved and only working a few hours on the front desk to generate the additional cash flow she needed. Needless to say, her client schedule filled up quickly. By reframing the purpose of her reception duties, she was able to feel gratitude for that position. I had no idea that what I was doing with my team, skills that came so naturally to me and that help people move out of stuckness, are known in professional coaching circles to be the competencies of *reframing, brainstorming,* and *active listening.*[1]

Soon, I realized that the things I was doing with the patients and the staff energized me. I loved it every time I could help someone see a new possibility. I was literally enjoying every single conversation enough that I began to see myself doing the same kind of work all day long without tiring, because it inspired me to my core. And, according to the feedback I received, the perk was that I was really good at it! As alluded to already, my research led me to learn that what I had been doing was a form of this thing called *coaching.*

The pure irony of that word was not lost on me! Yes, the word *coach* from the athletic world I no longer wished to be a part of, a word that had previously held negative associations for me, was the word that most aptly described the person I was becoming. Coaching was calling me, so I took a deep dive to find out more about what exactly coaching entails. The more I researched the profession, the more excited I got to think that this would be a truly exciting door of possibility for me.

Soon, I proposed that I get additional certification in professional coaching to the founder of the healing arts center, suggesting we could then formally offer it as one of our already out-of-the-box adjunct services.

At the same time, my creative friend and I rekindled our mutual interest in being together. He was flourishing in his new position in California, and he offered what seemed to be an "innocent" chance to catch up while he was back in New York for the holidays. But I believe we both knew what would happen when we saw each other. Our bond was very strong and sweet. Ultimately, we began visiting each other every other month and we made a point to speak by phone, text, or email every day, just to check in. My heart gave me a longing squeeze every time I thought of him. Within a year of his move to California, we were professing our love and discussing potential plans for me to move there with him. Needless to say, I expanded my coaching certification program search to include the state of California.

I was now fully following each exciting step as they appeared in front of me on this new path that had started with the question:

*What do I want my future to look like?*

I was feeling more peaceful and connected to Spirit/God/ Source/the Universe than I had since I was a child who believed in a God that loved everyone, especially children. My heart was leading me toward joining this creative friend in California, a person who, from the beginning, felt like home to me. And my heart seemed to be leading me toward an exciting career path that would enable me to make a positive impact on people's lives doing something I was both really good at and truly enjoyed.

So, I was at a crossroads and needed to look once more at potential future versions of my life. Should I: A) Stay by the lake very happy and content, or B) follow this exciting and scary path that was opening up in front of me? I did realize if I took the new path I would be scrutinized, criticized, and judged primarily because I was course correcting very late in the game. To my family, my behavior would seem unlike the predictable and reliable behavior the Responsible One had shown for so long. To almost everyone, I was giving up an honorable, financially stable career in medicine to pursue coaching, a profession that was not even formally recognized as a profession yet. Also, not only would I be making a third attempt at forming a serious intimate relationship, but I was moving across the country to do it without knowing anyone in the state I was going to except my boyfriend. I'm sure it looked like some sort of midlife crisis. And what if the relationship didn't work out? A legitimate concern, as technically, this relationship was still very new.

For me, even if it didn't work out with my creative friend, my heart's pull and the momentum in moving in this direction were undeniable. Although it was scary, I knew my choice was made. There was no doing this from that previously familiar perspective of "shoulds/shouldn'ts" or from trying to get someone's approval. The decision carried no rebellious energy in it, and no resistant energy either. It just felt like an opportunity door had swung wide open. Although there were no guarantees this would work out, the next step was to walk through the door I had discovered. Following this path through an open door was a step into showing up for my life as the most authentic version of myself so far.

The icing on this cake was knowing that I owned all my choices. I was co-creating a new chapter of my destiny. No more autopilot or living a story that other people had written for me.

Now that was empowering!

# CHAPTER 14

# *Thank You, iPEC*

*Parts of this chapter contain my interpretation of the copyrighted work of Bruce D. Schneider and the Institute for Professional Excellence in Coaching (iPEC).*

My search for a coaching certification program initially was interrupted by the move to California, and for several months, I was thankful to be able to still work remotely for the combined healing arts center. But it wasn't long into my resumed search that I stumbled on the website for the Institute for Professional Excellence in Coaching (iPEC). Immediately, I could see they had a message and spoke a language that resonated with me deeply. Their marketing materials spoke of coaches being trained in helping clients get to the core of their own blocks and limiting beliefs. They spoke of energy and of choice and of raising consciousness.[1]

The program was international and accredited. I knew if I was going to pursue coaching, I wanted to become masterful at it, so I had no doubt iPEC was the program for me. *Coincidentally*, they offered their weekend training modules in a location nearby us. Without hesitation, I signed up.

IPEC's curriculum included three immersion weekend modules spread out over six-plus months, and additional time after the third module to bring it all together and pass a certification exam. In the first weekend, a dynamic lead trainer stood in the center of the room and masterfully held our attention, asking us empowering questions that systematically helped us to uncover "the why" that brought all of us there. As she spoke, I started to see parts of myself in her—parts I could sense had yet to be tapped.

I fell immediately in love with their entire concept of Core Energy Coaching™. I loved that professional coaching was built around partnering with people who wanted to help themselves by assisting them in making conscious choices from a place of clarity.

*I loved the premise of Core Energy Coaching™ that with each conscious choice, we free ourselves from the confines of limited perspectives and gain access to experiencing whatever amazing life we want!*

Over those three days, I soaked in the materials presented and was prepared to be "all-in" for the curriculum ahead of us. I was excited to be learning skills with which I could help clients break free from self-critical core beliefs, while simultaneously being coached on this as well. I was even more excited to learn that, by the end of the program, as an Energy Leadership™ Index Master Practitioner (ELI-MP), I would be trained to not only "uncover" the energy that holds people back but also to facilitate the shifts that allow people to naturally rise to a more powerful version of themselves. My trainer spoke a lot about brilliance and of having infinite potential. And that weekend I had my first unforgettable light bulb moment.

While listening to our lead trainer, my mind wandered, and I began to ponder the notion of the human condition. I thought about all of the conditioning we as humans experience. I saw how normal it is for us to develop thought patterns in early childhood as we try to make sense of our world, then layer those thoughts with even more beliefs and habits that get imprinted onto our psyches by multiple outside influences (our parents, society, and so on) and that further reinforce those original thought patterns and beliefs.

As the trainer spoke, my mind kept coming back to this notion of conditioning. Hearing her use the word *conditioning* reminded me of the word *unconditional,* as in the concept of *unconditional love.* Then, instantly, I had a startling and joyous insight that made me want to jump up and interrupt her. (I didn't, of course, but the urge was that strong.)

With a deep inward breath, the thought that came was: *YES! Unconditional love! Love is all that is left when you remove all of that conditioning! It just IS!*

The following words perfectly express the realization I had during that moment:

*Your task is not to seek for love, but merely to seek and find all the barriers within yourself that you have built against it.*[2] This is either a quote from Rumi or from *A Course in Miracles*, but either way for me it captures my ah-ha moment's sentiment exactly.

In that moment of realization, I was seeing that our "conditioning" could be thought of as the equivalent to barriers we have built against love. Love itself is already here and it's easy to feel and know. We can naturally love, we come from love, and we would really only know love if we could remove all that conditioning. Love is without rules. Love is without exception. Love is without the __(blank)__ we have covered it with.

*Unconditional love is love without conditions.*

At that same moment, I was reminded of a peaceful baby looking in awe at the world around it. I was reminded of how I feel when I see sunlight reflecting off water. I was reminded of the sensation of warmth from my heart expanding through my chest when I feel that comforting Alchemy of Melting Cares.

What I didn't know during my light bulb moment was that this new awareness would take my thoughts and perspectives on life to an entirely other level. With this new awareness combined with what I was learning at the coach training program, I no longer wanted to look at the situations from my past, including all of the ones I've described so far in this book, as anything more than human conditioning. I also never wanted to think of the stories we create about our life situation as being so serious, so real, or so absolute. I wanted to keep reminding myself that my beliefs and feelings about the stories of our lives were just conditioning, because somehow that take on them gave me a sense of perfect clarity.

I could feel space opening up inside of me when I embraced the realization that Dad had just been living from his conditioning . . . and my exes from theirs . . . and Mom from hers . . . and me from mine. Who knows what conditioning or pain the little ones inside of Mom, Dad, or my current partner had experienced? Like little Lou, their little ones had subconsciously adopted personas and behaviors that were intended to help them get by and make sense of the world. This light bulb moment opened up space in me for compassion toward the little ones inside of others. It opened up space for me to experience unconditional love.

I could visualize the "little one" inside of Dad. As a young man growing up in the South during the '40s and '50s; or, as one of the few black athletes on a Midwestern college campus; or later, as a husband in an interracial marriage, what personas might Dad have had to adopt to feel safe or gain approval in his world? I could imagine his inner little one as he faced the fears and challenges of raising his own daughters alone. I could visualize part of his morning routine was putting on a mask of discipline and control as he got us up and out of the house to face the day. Meanwhile, his inner little one was only wanting to stay in bed and mourn the loss of his wife. I doubt he found the time to stop and contemplate what unconditional love could look like.

*This truth became crystal clear: We are*
*all doing the best that we can with the*
*conditioning we have and the limited awareness*
*we have access to in any moment.*

## Learning More from Lou

Everything about the immersion weekend had me believing I'd finally found something important I was meant to do.

*The experiences of my life had been*
*helping me hone and develop skills I could*
*one day use to help other people.*

I felt amazing, energized, and excited about positively impacting people's lives—and doing so without it being at my expense. I could make a difference without being drained or depleted. It did not require some sort of unnecessary over-functioning, sacrificing, or taking on the load of someone else's responsibilities. The work in itself was energizing. Every practice coaching session with my peers, the mentors, or with volunteers felt natural to me. It was as if I was born to do this.

Here was an opportunity to master techniques that would help me make an even bigger impact on people than I had imagined. It was almost too good to be true that I could be this happy merely thinking about a potential career. During each practice session in which I was the coach, I could see how I was intuitively coming up on the spot with new ways to use the basic skills taught to us, which surprised both my practice clients and me. From my personal history, I was drawing on the discipline of those track and field competitions, my medical career, and the comfort I'd gained from being in intimate, confidential spaces with patients at the combined healing arts center, as well as drawing from my painful and joyous relationship lessons, my religious background in multiple churches, the more recent spiritual discoveries I'd made, and the traumas that occurred in my youth.

I learned that one of my strongest skill sets as a coach was creating a safe and nonjudgmental space that facilitates the personal discovery process. I also discovered that this skill of holding a safe, nonjudgmental space for other people was coming so naturally to me because of Lou! While growing up in our frequently emotionally volatile home, instead of partaking in the drama, Lou was quietly listening, watching, and reading the subtle energy cues around her and becoming a master of discernment. This perceptivity was a strength I could bring to the table as a coach.

Finally, I was surprised to find that the technique of focused attention I had developed while running races for the university also turned out to be valuable for coaching. During those races, I had to learn to block out distractions and stay completely focused and present. Seconds sometimes felt like an eternity, as if time stood still. Eventually, I could simultaneously focus on the runner ahead of me and on my breathing and my running form. I had previously taken this skill set for granted, but with coaching, it was serving me very well.

*In summary, my "all too real" life education,
with its twists, turns, heartbreaks, and layering of
knowledge, would serve me very well as a coach.*

During my coach training, I often thought back to Lou reciting the Bible verse "All things [in the Universe] work together for good" as a strategy for coping with Mom's suicide. It was feeling more and more like this childhood mantra had not been naive after all.

My life experiences had coincidentally and perfectly equipped me for my new endeavor, and I was even more determined to become the most powerful and masterful transformational coach I could be. I would deep dive into the training required for this certification program and I wouldn't waste any opportunity to be of service. From then on, I lived and breathed coaching and anything that supported it.

I continued my new practices of listening to audiobooks, of going inward and being still and present, and of giving more loving attention to my inner child. I made it my priority to do more things that I thought both Lou and I would enjoy, such as more travel, more walks, taking dance classes, drawing, and attending live music events. I was now on a mission, and each step of my progress felt amazing!

I was determined to never ask anything of a client that I wasn't willing to do myself. And although, as noted earlier, my life history allowed me to go pretty "deep" already, I knew

I needed to be willing to go even further into exploring my core beliefs. In the name of being committed to "going there" and being all-in on this new chapter of my life that I was now consciously co-creating with Spirit/God/Source/the Universe, I signed up on my own to be professionally coached in addition to the immersion training I was receiving. There would be nowhere to run and I embraced that this time.

In preparation for the second immersion weekend, I decided to explore my core beliefs on my own, especially self-critical thoughts that stemmed from "not enough-ness." As a coach, I might briefly ask a client to consider what was the reason a core belief was created, but eventually they could acknowledge for themselves that it probably no longer made sense to hold onto this core belief, as the original reason was not presently valid—and they didn't have to carry old beliefs into their futures.

Because I had already done therapy for my own issues, I felt ready to look at myself as a coach would. The question at hand for me then became:

*How open am I to the possibility that we all have a choice either to keep the core beliefs that were indeed necessary once in the past or to choose new ones that may better serve us now in the present?*

This is the perfect time to admit to you that I intentionally labeled Lou's childhood personas with names such as the Obedient One and the Responsible One for the sake of making a point in this chapter of the book. There is a well-studied notion of labeling (or naming) aspects of our behavior as a means of dis-identifying with an experience (or an intense emotion or thought). This enables us to place some distance between us and what we perceive in order to dissipate its emotional charge and influence over us.

A team of researchers in the psychology department at the University of California, Los Angeles, conducted a brain-imaging study that showed "how putting negative feelings into words (affect labeling) can help regulate negative experience, a process that may ultimately contribute to better mental and physical health."[3] In essence, as a negative emotional charge diminishes, we are able to view negative critical thoughts and feelings with more objectivity and curiosity.

Researchers studying vipassana meditation found similar results from the same practice. "Labeling helps us to perceive clearly the actual qualities of our experience, without getting immersed in the content. It develops mental power and focus."[4]

Similarly, in *Energy Leadership, Transforming Your Workplace and Your Life from the Core,* iPEC founder Bruce D. Schneider describes four primary energy blocks. In his words, the fourth of these is "fear that you are not enough, the inner critic, or what is sometimes called a gremlin."[5] He recommends naming your gremlins to diminish their power.

Bruce Schneider writes:

"The easiest way to banish a gremlin is to reveal its face. Once revealed, actually giving the gremlin a name helps to separate it from you."[6]

What was my gremlin? I certainly still heard plenty of self-critical messages running through my mind. It felt a lot like I had been bullying myself. Now, not only did I observe the familiar personas of the Obedient One, the Responsible One, and the Workhorse in myself, I also met my biggest inner critic, whom I labeled My Bully.

I knew right away that My Bully had been with me for years—certainly surfacing somewhere in childhood. I could hear it telling me all the ways I (or others) "should have" behaved differently in any given situation. I recalled there was once a disgruntled ex-coworker that told me she felt bullied by me at times. Now it made perfect sense that there may have indeed been many times My Bully showed itself to others in the name of "constructive feedback" or "tough love." My Bully also told me how defective and ugly I was because I was the only family member with acne. Worse, it often called me *gross* because the skin condition was cystic acne.

My Bully repeatedly told me I should give up on the "fantasy life" of coaching and go back to practicing medicine as a doctor because I was "too old to change now," and I would "no longer be respected." Furthermore, My Bully was certain I would never amount to anything with all the medical school debt "dragging along behind me like a ball and chain." My Bully tried to convince me many times that my creative boyfriend would eventually see there were hotter, younger girls out there and leave me for them, so I should just leave him already and get the pain over with before that happens.

Let me just say, once I clearly became aware of this voice, I realized that the voice of My Bully in my head was intense.

Then one day, during my daily practice of stillness, I attempted on my own to see if I could try to actually visualize My Bully, as I had previously done with my little Lou. *Warning!* Do not try this on your own without the assistance of a professional! In hindsight, it might not have been the best idea to do this all by myself, because it was frightening. But I was in the habit of jumping in to try new things without much forethought, so I went with the impulse and did it.

Immediately, as I tried to imagine what My Bully could look like, I felt a chill run up my spine and a sense of darkness come over the room. The feeling was as if I were a child in the dark with something intensely scary hovering right next to my face on the right. I held my breath and tried not to move. My entire body stiffened in fear and my heart raced in panic. Did you ever see the movie *Alien*? If so, you may recall the scene where Sigourney Weaver has to hold her breath and remain still as the alien's slimy jaw and teeth pass inches from her face. It's nerve wracking and the entire audience braces themselves along with her.

That was my first inclination and brand-new insight into how scary life must have been for little Lou from her perspective. As a child, she was incapable of explaining the chaotic and often volatile world around her. Like inventing her other protective identities, Lou created My Bully to ensure she toed the line. All she knew from her childhood perspective was that the consequences would be dire if she did not.

The intensity of the "brace myself" feeling was very familiar now that I was aware of it. Looking back, I could also see how many times I had felt the energy like that of My Bully in those around me: for example, when I received that stare of disgust from the team trainer at the university and every time I was in fear that Dad's wrath was set loose.

To my surprise, when I was able to look at My Bully with enough distance and curiosity, I understood clearly the even more obvious reason that Lou had created it. It was there to stop and protect Lou from saying or doing what she *really* wanted to do! Had she possessed the strength of a gladiator or thought she would be safe enough to get away with it, Lou would have yelled at that team trainer or thrown something toward Dad and watched it smash on the wall behind him to see how he liked it. Or she might have squeezed instead of stroked her childhood friend's brother's "appendage" as if her hand were a vice grip!

I could see that, in those situations, without having had any role models for empowerment, My Bully was trying to keep Lou from getting kicked off of the track team, avoiding injury, and since she was clearly much too small to win a plate-smashing fight with Dad, stop her from doing something potentially harmful to herself. My Bully was also there stopping Lou from getting thrown out of that brother's basement into the street in the middle of the night to walk home alone with who knows who or what else was lurking.

My Bully's core belief was that the act of bullying Lou was indeed in her best interest! It believed Lou would be safest if she would stay quiet and small in a world that didn't appear safe.

My Bully made sure Lou stuck to the rules and roles that would please everyone around her. Most importantly, my Bully knew that what was even scarier to me than My Bully itself was the core belief that I was nothing. The belief that I was walked away from and therefore unworthy of even a mother's love. I could see that's why I (little Lou) had created this harshly critical inner voice.

I was also finally seeing that, even though I was now an empowered and competent adult, My Bully was still going along doing its job as usual. In the name of protecting me, it was looking to scare me into submission with critical and defeating thoughts.

*Meanwhile, I, a full-grown adult, hadn't even been conscious of the fact that I was still listening to this childhood creation!*

The question naturally was: *How could I, as an adult who no longer needs that kind of help, visualize My Bully now?* When I asked this, an image quickly came to mind of a small cartoon version of the alien in the movie *Alien,* growling through its tiny teeth up at me. I literally belly laughed at the visual of that cute little guy!

### The Weekend of No "Stories"

I shared the story of meeting My Bully with the professional coach I hired and explained how he had become a cute cartoon once I was conscious that he was a child's creation. I told her that I could clearly see now that my core beliefs were just stories. Creating enough space between myself and My Bully's story had allowed me to get curious and look for other possible messages I wanted to be telling myself to replace the mean ones My Bully told me. This was what I had guided patients and staff at the combined healing arts center to do so many times, and now I was being guided to this place myself—the place of seeing that the scary story is just one of many possibilities. I shared that I was gifting myself the opportunity to step back and choose which of the other possible stories/beliefs were really the ones I wanted to influence my decisions.

While being coached, I experienced another transformative insight. It was intense. To loosely paraphrase, I recall our exchange going something like this:

Coach: "Let's put aside the story that you were being bullied by your dad and then later by your own thoughts and go into the feelings associated with the story. Where in your body do you feel it when you think of your dad bullying you and/or the Bully-Alien at your face?"

Me: "A tight chest, tight jaw, holding my breath, and racing heart. A fear of something terrible happening if I did anything wrong or didn't do exactly as he said."

Coach: "Yes, I hear you saying your body is constricting and there's intense fear. Are there other sensations in your body when you believe the story that something horrible could happen to you?"

Me: "Lower in my body, there's a nauseous pit in my stomach, and behind that, a deep emptiness that I remember feeling that night my mother committed suicide."

The coach nodded her head, inviting me to keep talking but remaining quiet and focused on me. Briefly, I became aware that my hands were shaking, and tears were running down my cheeks. I felt vulnerable in front of her but was still willing to keep going and turned my focus back on nausea and the pit in my stomach.

Me: "The nausea is like when you want to vomit at seeing something horribly indescribable."

Coach: "What is the nausea telling you that is so indescribable?"

Me: "That my parents were supposed to love me, but they didn't."

Coach: "If your parents didn't love you, what does that say about you?"

Me: "That they must hate me. That I am unlovable."

Coach: "And the feeling in the pit of emptiness, what is the message associated with that?"

Me: "It feels like nothingness. Complete resignation. I am nothing."

The room was quiet and still. I stopped crying and shaking as the coach and I felt that pit together. The coach remained still and focused on me. Although my eyes were closed and there was a feeling of dark emptiness, I understood that she was there in the dark with me. Mutually, our attention was on the awareness of this deep, dark place that had been exposed.

We were exposing the darkness in me to the light.

Coach (After an uncertain amount of time): "I am hearing you say that you believe you are nothing."

Me: "Yes. Wait, no. Even as I start to answer you . . . even as I start to say yes, that there is a part of me in the pit of my stomach that believes I am nothing, I can feel another part of me that KNOWS that's not true."

Coach: "Well, what IS true?"

Me:

*"I am full of light and love. I have an opportunity to fulfill a purpose: to let my light shine as a gift to others to help them see their own."*

The words rolled off my tongue from a place of certainty that all was well. I knew any belief other than this was just another story, just more mental conditioning. I stood there in stillness, feeling a combination of joy, peace, warmth, and love while the room remained quiet. I opened my eyes to see the coach beaming at me with a huge smile. For me, there was only the perfection of the moment of letting go of other stories and embodying my pure truth.

My coach asked me if I'd like to keep going but I chose instead to end our session there and continue basking in this new internal silence and peace. It was surreal to be without the noise of my mind or any residual chatter coming from beliefs of unworthiness. The awareness of being a part of and infused with the Essence that is in everything made everything other than that disappear.

My creative friend-turned-life-partner had been away visiting his family that weekend and I was grateful to go home to an empty apartment where I could keep experiencing this peaceful internal silence without trying to explain it. I was super aware of everything I was doing, and also aware that there were neither associated stories nor an internal commentary about my activities. Nothing was sticking. This was very different than anything I had experienced before, and I didn't want it to end. Eventually, an intermittent thought arrived: *Wow, it has been X number of hours now without my own thoughts popping in!* But then I drifted right back into silence. It was only an instant of acknowledgment.

By evening, another thought popped in: *Wow, I'm still just sitting here by myself in my apartment feeling peaceful in silence. Maybe this is not normal behavior and I should try to watch TV.* I grabbed the remote and flipped through the channels, but I couldn't get lost in any of the stories. I was aware of everything that was happening. Simultaneously, I was aware of sitting in the room, of looking at the TV screen, of watching actors telling a story, of the light from the street lamp coming in through a crack in the drapes, and of the buzz from a fan in the corner. My mind was otherwise silent. *Hmm, the TV stories aren't sticking either,* I observed. I turned off the TV and closed my eyes to continue basking in peaceful silence.

Before I drifted to sleep that night, I had a light feeling as if I were floating through outer space. Normally I would have analyzed it and wondered what it meant. I tried to start a conversation with myself about the image, yet every thought I tried to conjure just wouldn't stick. It was like these thoughts were coming to my attention from behind me, almost fully formed, but then would just fall away. I finally stopped trying to think and drifted to sleep.

Since my partner wasn't going to be home until Monday, I spent three days in this space of peaceful silence. I now call those days the *Weekend of No Stories*. If there was someone talking to me, like the cashier at the supermarket, I would listen to what she was saying with an intense awareness not only of her words but also everything else occurring at the same time. After people spoke, or after my replies, I would return to complete silence in my head.

Gradually, as I interacted with more people, read emails, and returned to my usual routine, the usual chatter in my head returned and the stories began to stick again. These were stories like, "I need to get this done by a certain time," or "This is what I should do next." I also experienced judgments, like wondering if I looked okay in a certain dress. You know, the usual mind chatter we have in our heads. And while intentionally stopping the chatter to meditate, visualize, or practice being still, it helped to remember that the chatter was just my human conditioning and that we humans love our stories.

Ever since that amazing Weekend of No Stories, whenever interactions with people were painful or uncomfortable, recalling the phrase *It's all conditioning and stories* has helped me have more clarity and peace in my professional and personal relationships. As my own conditioning was reflected to me over and over again in my relationship with my partner, our connection deepened. Most of what used to be sources of discord dissolved.

I watched the two of us growing together and flourishing to the point that we literally cheered ourselves on! We'd come out of productive arguments celebrating, "Wow, we are really good for each other!" or "Did I ever tell you how much I love us?!?" My new awareness was that my beloved had the same Essence flowing through him as I had. Once I was able to see this, the recognition allowed me to trust him and relax into intimate partnership with him. I had never been capable of fully trusting a man before, but here I was finally just appreciating the gift of being able to be in this moment on the journey of life together.

*I was opening up more space for compassion and for the capacity to love bigger than I could imagine.*

## Learning to Free My Energy

Being a student really was so much more exciting this time around since there was an added layer of passion and choice to it and the added bonus of my personal healing. I had made the controversial decision to leave medicine and pursue coach training at iPEC, and I'm so happy I did. I knew that if I could learn to do for other people what I was learning to do for myself, I would really be able to make a positive contribution to so many people's lives.

At iPEC, we were also introduced to an assessment tool iPEC calls the Energy Leadership Index (ELI). The ELI helps us gain awareness of our personal stories and conditioning. It's intended for use with clients, but since we were still students, we were using it to look at ourselves. After we took the ELI, we were debriefed on the results. The results were the revelation of a unique energy combination that an individual utilizes in daily life and another reactive energy pattern that we habitually fall into when we're feeling stressed out. Having wasted too many years on autopilot, it was fascinating to become more conscious of the ways I was expending energy to maintain stories and perceptions that weren't actually serving me. It was equally motivating to learn how to free that energy so it would be available to use toward creating a life that was more aligned with my vision for myself.

My take-home during this combination period of coach training and real-life training was that my energy, options, and decisions become limited and restricted when one of the following conditions is met:

- ♦ When I have complete attachment to a story,
- ♦ When I make a judgment about a given situation, or
- ♦ When I identify with the views of a persona I am embodying (for example, the Bully or the Obedient One).

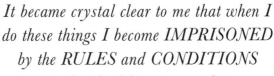

*It became crystal clear to me that when I do these things I become IMPRISONED by the RULES and CONDITIONS associated with my perceptions.*

On the other hand, my energy is expansive and free, and *"all things work together"* effortlessly in my favor, when I remember:

- ♦ That all of it is stories and conditioning,

- That the one perspective is just one of multiple possible realities,
- That life itself is an opportunity to discover and allow and experience, and
- That I am free to be open and radiate the love and light within me.

*When I remember to simply follow my heart's desire, or let love lead, I am free to co-create any life I wish to experience. The choice is mine.*

I was already beginning to see, feel, know, and experience the freedom and flow of following my heart's desires, and I wanted to keep up that momentum and see where it took me. So far, my heart was taking me on a wonderful, amazing ride.

Professionally, I was now even more determined to help my future coaching clients in the most powerful, impactful, brightest, lovingly transformational way I possibly could. I kept up my education with ongoing self-studies and audiobooks, I attended online workshops and I volunteered to coach anyone and everyone who wanted coaching (often free of charge) provided we mutually felt it was a fit. I also used personal challenges, as they arose, as opportunities to coach myself and see which of the tools in my coaching "toolbox" proved reliably the most powerful.

# CHAPTER 15

# An Introduction to Look With Me™ Coaching

I spent several months and considerable effort designing the coaching system that I still use today in my private coaching practice. This combines the coaching tools that have had the most powerful impact on me and on my clients. It has three elements.

- ♦ **LOOK = Intentionally Focused Attention.** Using active and intuitive listening, I am there beside my client as we intentionally focus our attention toward the part(s) inside of them that owns a specific viewpoint/perspective. Usually it's the viewpoint giving them the most grief, the most resistance, or keeping them stuck. Then, like patting an empty seat beside me, I invite my client to look together with me from an elevated (or bird's-eye) view at their "inner little one" and the stories that little one has been acting out. From positioning ourselves in this new view, we're also able to create a figurative separation between A) Them and B) the Little Inner Part of Them that they've previously not been seeing or listening to. Once the slightest distance has been created, light is allowed to shine into this newly created space between. For instance, consider the examples throughout this book demonstrating my stepping back from only seeing through my adult-conditioned view and allowing a light to shine on how the little Lou part of me had been seeing things.

♦ **WITH = Being Present with Ourselves and with Nonjudgmental Curiosity.** As the coach, I support a nonjudgmental space in our sessions that allows my client and their "little one" to feel safe enough to be seen and open up an actual dialogue. Once in dialogue, those previously unheard, unseen, and/or abandoned inner "parts" receive deep validation by finally feeling the loving, focused attention and presence they've craved. The client by this time usually, and finally, feels free to tell their true core belief story, share what lights them up, and discover their heart's desires for their relationship or their business or their life. This leads to their personal creation of the next step, ME.

♦ **ME = Show yourself ME-Love by creating your own Signature Self-Love Formula.** Here, the client learns to formally gift herself/himself with the long overdue love and attention she/he has been missing. I find this the most beautiful part of our coaching sessions, because people are so often unaware of what ways they have been abandoning and neglecting themselves, just as I had been. The client finds this special Signature Self-Love Formula on her/his own. The formula comes as a unique gift or practice to fulfill and honor the neglected needs and desires of her/his inner little one. My clients learn, as I did, that loving the child within us is the doorway to full-on unconditional love. "Show ME-Love," says their inner little ones!

Time and time again, this process has shown that once we've experienced unconditional love for ourselves and we can no longer wait, and instead leap at the opportunity to gift ourselves with fulfilling our dreams, we are set free to play and to experience having what we want out of our lives and our relationships.

In my experience, as people commit to gifting themselves their own self-love practices that speak specifically to their inner little one, the *coincidences* in their lives start to happen on an increasingly rapid scale. I attribute this to the fact that they begin resonating with (instead of resisting) what Spirit/God/Source/the Universe has wanted for them all along! In my personal experience, Spirit/God/ Source/the Universe wants it for us just because we want it. Achieving our heart's desires often miraculously has the ripple effect of being an example and an inspiration to others and allows for even more opportunities of growth, expansion, joy, and love.

Here are hypothetical examples of what occurs during a Look With Me™ Coaching session.

In a session, a client might tell me: "*My partner always does X and it is just so infuriating!*"

After listening with intense presence to the client's associated stories surrounding their infuriating situation, the client starts to feel a sense of deep validation from just being truly heard and understood. The validation creates an opening for me to ask something along the lines of this:

*If it were possible that you repeatedly felt infuriated as a child by something very similar, what name could you give the childhood identity that would be telling me this same story?*

If the client can't separate enough from that identity to give it its own unique name, I ask the client to try telling me which Disney character (or superhero or metaphor) it reminds them most of when they are telling their story in this way.

In this specific case, part of the client's story might sound like: "My partner always watches as I not only work all day but then I come home to do everything around the house; meanwhile, he never lifts a finger to help. It's just so infuriating!" The client decides that story actually sounds a lot like Cinderella's story. So, we'd name that inner little part of them Cinderella to start.

Or if the client says: "My partner always treats me like a child and doesn't let me have any fun and tells me I'll never grow up and it's so infuriating!" we might decide that sounds most like Peter Pan's story. So, we'd name that childhood inner little one Peter Pan, at least to start.

Naming the inner child character who is speaking to us begins creating the metaphorical distance that is needed to free our energy from being so tied up in playing out these stories we've created. It helps my clients to be more aware of the subconscious persona within them that is holding their current hurt or angered point of view/perspective, just like how I described becoming aware of my different "personas." The space created by the separation allows "the light" to get in so we can see the bigger picture clearer.

The safer a coaching space is that I have created for the client, the more I am able to hear the voices of these different childhood characters inside of them. Sometimes I actually get an image in my mind's eye of their inner little one "acting out" these characters like roles in a well-rehearsed movie. And as was the case for me in my own life, these roles get repeated and repeated—it may be a different scene (home, work, relationships, parenting), but the "script" tends to be the same! Yet, ultimately, with the spotlight now shining on these inner little characters, the client can Look With Me™ at them from a lens of curiosity and compassion, as if we are watching lovable children playing roles.

*Awareness arises that these childhood creations*
*are simply using this current uncomfortable*
*situation in your life as an opportunity to*
*get your attention and speak to you.*

Let me give you another example of how this might play out while in a coaching session. With permission, one of my clients has allowed me to share more specifics here to paint a clearer picture. This client eventually was able to successfully name and identify four different inner little characters:

- Character A was her work persona.
- Character B was the persona she took on when she was in the presence of her family.
- Character C was the persona she brought with her to our coaching sessions, who she also would show to a rare close friend.
- Character D was the persona she admitted she was ashamed of, who usually felt depressed and scared at night when she was alone.

These four characters/personas/identities used distinctly different languages to express themselves. Furthermore, the roles they played were so clearly defined that all I would have to do to bring awareness to the client was to say something like, "Ahhh, I think this sounds like I story I have heard Character B tell us before," and my client would immediately laugh at how amazingly easy it was for her to instantly shape-shift into one of these characters, depending upon the situation and in what way she was being triggered. The more my client witnessed these characters (created in childhood) and intentionally allowed them to fully express themselves, the more compassion and love she found she was capable of giving to them.

During our time together, she made great strides in loving and validating all four discovered versions of herself; she invited them to teach her how to be a fuller, more complete expression of herself. At the time of writing this book, she reported that she was falling in love with more of herself and felt noticeably less shame. She had also found more joy in her work and her personal life, as she continues to discover and reclaim forgotten and neglected parts of herself. One of these included rediscovering her childhood love of playing the piano, which she now does more regularly as a means of expressing herself and being creative.

CHAPTER 16

# *Cosmic Coach Conversations*

I am sharing these coaching "secrets" because I've personally seen that even the smallest shifts in perspective or the application of a new practice in self-love can yield tremendous, life-changing results. For instance, even if the small commitment to make time to be present with yourself without running to do the next thing on your to-do list sounds too simple to make a difference, it may be the exact kind of loving attention you've craved or needed for a long time.

Let me also take the time to remind you again, if deeply painful feelings surface that feel overwhelming, please enlist the assistance of a therapist to support you. Many wounded and abandoned parts of us need to be provided a safe, supportive space in which to be heard. Simply being willing to give those parts of yourself attention and seeking professional guidance as you do so is a huge step in the direction of loving life and living a life you love.

Following the first step of just being willing, another important next step on the path to loving yourself enough to gift yourself an amazing life is to stop running away from, neglecting, and abandoning yourself. As you've now seen through my own firsthand account, abandoning yourself may involve always looking externally or looking outside of yourself for others to give you what you need and possibly never received as a child. That is not to say that someone outside of you, like a sibling, a close friend, or a partner, won't be able to meet your needs. It is just that those who you've surrounded yourself with are merely a reflection of what degree you've chosen to provide for your own well-being. The more loving you are to yourself and the more you enjoy meeting your own needs, the more you'll attract others who are loving and enjoy meeting needs as well.

What I have learned from my own experience and firmly believe is this: The moment we shift from looking outward to looking inward, we dial into the energy that will effortlessly flow more loving attention to us. I've learned that the more of a practice you make it to give and receive self-care and the longer you stay there in the energy of self-love, the more you invite others with the same desire to love and be loving into your life.

*It's like inviting Spirit/God/Source/*
*the Universe and those around you*
*to give you exactly what you want,*
*by actually wanting it enough to*
*be willing to give it to yourself.*

Because it's important, let me clarify here again that I am not saying your needs cannot be met by others and should only be met by you. What I am saying is that I am convinced the key to experiencing a full life lies in opening up to the idea that there may be an infinite number of ways to be loved and have your needs met.

*Inviting the gifts of loving people and*
*resources into your current awareness*
*begins with dialing into the experience*
*of your own loving attention.*

With this in mind, please now allow me to share with you my own personal practice of self-coaching that can be done anywhere. This practice has been transformative for me and always gives me the rewards of

A) quality time with myself, and

B) allowing the parts of me in need to be heard and loved.

During my own journey self-coaching was a vital part of developing and putting my coaching skills to practice. Self-coaching also was an opportunity to connect with the place within me that is connected to Spirit/God/Source/the Universe and to get clear on what I want. It was a means for me to discern what choice was the best way for me to move forward next. It's also my favorite practice for getting myself unstuck in a pinch—with the added benefit of shining a warm light into any lingering cold, dark, lonely places within me.

My specific style of a self-coaching is to foster a dialogue between myself (often as little Lou or another newly discovered character she created) and what I call my *Cosmic Coach*. The term "Cosmic Coach" came to me while learning of what iPEC calls our "Higher Coach." *Higher Coach* comes from one of iPEC's foundation principles. Specifically: *We each have a Higher Coach.*[1]

My Cosmic Coach is, by my definition, speaking to me directly from its connection with Spirit/God/Source/the Universe. If that idea is too woo-woo for your comfort, maybe you can consider it a dialogue between the "You of Your Current Perspective" and the "You Residing in the Wiser, Usually Untapped, Parts of Your Brain." This specific self-coaching practice gets more powerful the more you do it, but since we cannot get practiced at anything if we don't start somewhere, I encourage you to try at least once or twice, if you are so inclined, before you give up on it.

To begin a self-coaching Cosmic Coach Conversation, or CCC, as I now call this technique, I go somewhere to be alone with a journal, a blank sheet of paper, or a blank doc on my laptop. Beforehand, I tell the important people around me that I am doing a coaching project, so I will be unavailable for an hour or so. Sometimes this also looks like me waking up in the middle of the night feeling anxious about something and heading to the couch with my iPhone Notes app so I can keep the lights off.

I've always begun these CCC sessions with the format of "Me" making a statement, and in response, my "CC" asking me a question. I literally write the words *Me* and *CC.* Here is a sample dialogue.

Me: *A statement describing exactly what I am challenged with, anxious about, feeling stuck on, and so on.*

CC: *A free-flowing, curious, open-ended question as the response to Me.*

When it is time to have your CC ask you a question, allow whatever (usually commonsense) question to come to you without even thinking about it first. I write the first question that pops into my awareness. Open-ended questions seem to be the norm, but sometimes you might also be asking a yes/no question.

The dialogue begins like this and then continues as long as it takes until there's a sense of closure and clarity around the problem I was having. At the end, I typically feel a relaxed confidence about whatever action I wish to take or whichever direction I wish to move in. Middle-of-the-night sessions usually end with a feeling of melted cares and falling asleep.

To further share examples with you, I have pulled out old personal journal entries from a couple of my favorite CCC sessions done shortly after becoming a certified professional coach.

## Sample CCC Session 1: Disidentification from the Doctor

A big challenge arose for me almost immediately after getting certified as a professional coach. I was facing an important question: "OK, so how do I now explain to my family and peers that I have given up (oops, excuse me, 'retired early from') medicine and now, instead, I am pursuing my passion for this thing called *coaching?*"

I was no longer in possession of the certainty that comes with being a physician, the certainty that I could always find a high-income job, pay my bills, and meet my basic needs. This "coaching thing," as noted earlier, was not even a recognized profession yet. Although I knew the transformation within my own life as a result of coaching had been positive and powerful, I was not yet certain if this would be a sustainable source of income. My partner worried about this all along, but I, too, was now beginning to worry.

Yet, when I took a closer look, the truth was that as the Doctor I wasn't really even all that secure. Although my earning potential had been large, the cost for me personally was even larger. I was beginning to understand that my identification with the Doctor had not just been about having an obvious reliable career choice well suited for someone like me who believed she was responsible for everyone else's well-being. It was also about having an instant source of immediate approval from the outside world; it was a perfect shield from ever needing to face my fears of disapproval.

Finally, I discovered that the biggest cost to me was about how I was using it as an excuse not to actually live my life or fully experience the things of life like play, joy, or motherhood.

I had substituted the adage "A Doctor's Work Never Ends" for the cultural adage of "A Woman's Work Never Ends" and then used this as an excuse to become a workaholic. I used what felt like insurmountable medical school bills and credit card debt as an excuse to remain head down at my desk and hide in my work for years on end. Although I had managed to decrease my medical school debt from being roughly $160,000 in the hole to $45,000, I was very aware I was still "in the hole," and further believing I would always be stuck down there.

*Unknown to me, all of those years I had been suffering from the ailment that life begins at some elusive "One Day."*

As the Doctor, I believed that "One Day" when I could get out of the negative and reach a solid ground above me, that's when my life would finally begin. That's when I would finally be happy. So, I preferred not to even look up and just kept focused on digging myself out of the hole. Keeping my head down protected me from the painful reminder of believing I was chained to a life of indebtedness.

With further introspection, and during my coach training, I saw that I had spent years believing I owed my life to someone else. As I child, I believed I owed blind obedience to Dad for not turning his back on me and my sister as Mom did when she killed herself. In school, I believed I owed my body to a university's athletic team in exchange for the school paying for my education. Then I believed I owed all the money earned by sacrificing the majority of my time and my most fertile years to paying off the debt of the privilege to become the Doctor. This belief was reinforced by knowing that the majority of physicians I encountered were still in debt; or, if not, were still a single setback away from financial catastrophe. (We all paid an obnoxious amount of money to malpractice insurance to protect us from that prospect.)

I had finally decided that if I were to change the current trajectory of my future, I had to pick up my head, look around, and see where I really wanted to be in order to make real change. It was very clear that I would not be returning to the medical field, but in making that announcement, I did have to address the valid questions that I would be asked by the skeptics about my decision, such as: "How will you make money while waiting for your new coaching endeavor to provide a sustainable income?"

The first obvious and practical answer was that, until I had a regular flow of paying coaching clients, it would make the most sense to have another source of income. The most commonsense next step then became to work at any job I could find and do easily while simultaneously building my coaching practice.

But that's when I hit the block. Doing any job other than coaching did not appeal to me. Not at all. I had finally found what I absolutely loved, and what I could do for hours on end tirelessly, so there was no desire or motivation to do anything else. I felt stuck having these new amazing skills and no consistent flow of clients and dwindling savings. On top of that, this lack of certainty was beginning to place a toll on my otherwise amazing relationship.

With the vision of my future as the overarching intention, I jumped into a CCC with myself, focusing on my resistance to getting a new job. I wanted to see with clarity what internal messages I was likely ignoring that were getting in my way of being all-in and making the necessary changes. I did suspect the place my Cosmic Coach would take me would be straight to the conditioned beliefs that came from having grown up in a family all too familiar with debt and/or scraping by. My role models taught by example how to only live paycheck to paycheck. From this perspective, here is how my self-coaching session unfolded. (Again, for reference, CC = Cosmic Coach; Me = the Me with the limited perspective.)

Me: "I really need to make money and get a job since my coaching business is too new and just getting started, but I have no interest in doing anything else."

CC: "What would be at least one reason for not wanting to change your current state?—the state of not currently having sustainable income while you are waiting for more coaching clients or more coaching projects?"

Me: "Hmmm. It would make sense to me that I would be blocking potential sources of income due to a fear of getting back to work, where work = time lost or work = compromising my passions again. But if I keep thinking about why I might not want to go back to work, I guess I could see from the perspective of that inner part of me that is finally happy to have someone in my life who clearly is willing AND wanting to take care of me. That inner part of me keeps telling the story that *no family member ever demonstrated they fully wanted to take care of me, but instead seemed to only do so under a sense of obligation.* That story feels deeply sad. So, in turn, I can see that I have likely been spending much of my life staying in debt just waiting for someone finally to *love me enough* to take care of me…potentially waiting for someone to offer to free me from debt."

CC: "What exactly does *being taken care of* mean to you or give you?"

Me: "*Being taken care of* means that it allows me to RELAX, to no longer WORRY about whether my basic needs will be met. It means to no longer spend so much time in survival mode and to no longer feel the burden of RESPONSIBILITY of meeting my own needs or anyone else's."

CC: "What burden comes with responsibility and meeting your own needs?"

Me: "*Needs can only be met with suffering and self-sacrifice.* Ohh. I can still hear that depressing message inside of me somewhere. It feels like a kind of unspoken mantra and I can hear it in much of the world around me as well. But I no longer want to believe this. Instead, I want my new mantra to be:

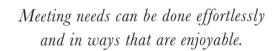

*Meeting needs can be done effortlessly*
*and in ways that are enjoyable.*

Me: "I'm seeing now that I've attached this old self-imposed definition of meeting needs onto a future potential income opportunity."

CC: "What can you do now, do today, to relax and love yourself enough to want to meet your own needs?"

Me: "*Hmmm* . . . What is relaxing and effortless that I could do today to show myself I love myself?

1. I can apply my fun practice of asking myself 'what do I *want* to do?' and then do that.

2. It would feel effortless and more loving to make a point of being more appreciative every time I receive money instead of my usual focusing on how it is still 'not enough' to pay off the debt in full. Ahhh [light bulb]… I have not really been that grateful!

3. It would feel effortless to apply the new practice of visualization and do as Dr Wayne Dyer said—'*contemplate yourself surrounded by the conditions you wish to produce*'[2]— and thereby shifting my focus and opening up my awareness to the multiple resources and possibilities that are likely already around me and right in front of me that I haven't been seeing because I've only instead been focused on the worry of not having enough! Ha! Boom! [It felt sort of like I'd been hit by a cosmic wisdom bolt!]

"I can also feel now that I DO love myself enough and I do WANT to take care of me! The image I see now is future ME thanking ME for not only wanting to take care of me but looking for fun, effortless opportunities to actually take care of me!" (More exciting cosmic wisdom light rays!)

And with this conclusion from my self-coaching session, I took the first step toward getting out of my own way to practically and financially taking care of myself! I was both empowered and inspired to come up with a list of ways I could look for fun jobs or side jobs that were complementary to coaching that would also bring in income. I also decided I wanted to find a job that still gave me plenty of time to build my coaching practice. Finally, I used the resources already at my disposal. In this case, I referred to Tony Robbins's *Unleash the Power Within* program materials and bought his book *Money*.

Robbins's book *Money* inspired me to open a high-interest savings account online immediately and to let go of my previous excuse, "I have to pay off debt first before I can save money or look for ways to invest." Needless to say, my savings started to increase almost effortlessly.

I know, I know. I can already feel your disappointment and see you squirming as you read this. How could someone so intelligent have been so clueless about money and savings for so long? But I am sharing my journey, even the parts that bring up shame, in full transparency and authenticity to free a potential reader who might need to hear this advice, too.

### "Ahhh…I can help her now"

Meanwhile, one of my childhood friends had mentioned months before that she might want me to coach her, but she wasn't sure when she'd be ready to commit to purchasing a package. I could also sense a hesitation within myself since I knew for me to agree to coach her, I would only want it to be in full confidence and without any inkling of hesitation that I would be the correct person to help her. When I concluded the preceding CCC session, this friend immediately popped into my mind. I remembered that she had a similar underlying issue as mine of "waiting for someone else to take care of her" and essentially not really wanting to take care of herself, at least not financially. The awareness came to me in that instant and I almost said out loud to myself, "Ahhh, yes, that was the hesitation. I can help her now." Literally the next day, she *coincidentally* sent me a message saying she wanted to sign up for the nine-week coaching package.

To generate momentum, I embraced searching for a part-time side job while I continued the rest of my focus on all things coaching. Clients still came in only gradually, so it was useful to have begun the search for that side job. What I hadn't realized was that being so happy to "focus on all things coaching," I had now started to ever so slightly shift my focus away from my creative friend, now partner. Because I had been so used to being independent, I had not been sharing my coaching plans or my issues with finances with the man I called my partner. Previous significant others were typically too interested in their own endeavors and "extracurricular activities" to express interest in hearing about mine, so it had never occurred to me that my new partner might want to know about those other parts of my life, like decisions about career or finances. Also, being raised in a single-parent home for most of my childhood, there was no model for considering how career decisions or finances would mentally or emotionally affect a partner.

Well, one of the traits I admired most about my creative friend was his transparency and being able to call me out on my BS. And call me out he did. He showed me that it looked like nothing short of pure hypocrisy to be referring to him as my "partner," but then not keeping him in the loop of major life decisions. From his view, I was not acting like a partner who could contribute to a stable financial future together at all. Hearing him share this perspective was a completely crushing shock to me, and I could 100 percent see his perspective. His observation made perfect sense, and it was deeply painful to think I could have dismissed his needs, but I welcomed the wake-up call that it was time to redefine partnership to be more aligned with all of my new awareness.

The funny thing was that I was sooo used to being the one in a relationship who called the other person on his BS. Just imagine what living with the Responsible One would have looked like. I was rarely ever the one to make mistakes. But perhaps needless to say, those relationships were not true partnerships. And here, with someone I deeply loved and wanted to be my permanent life partner, I was the one to be "irresponsible," and in this way, not the most appealing of prospects for a future partner.

My previous lack of interest in getting a job (the block that I did the self-coaching to investigate) had looked to him like I wasn't even considering a potential future together where I could be a contributing partner, but as if I were just going through the

motions. Here I was, believing myself to be a powerful transformational coach in the making, and yet I had somehow missed the
essential step of "checking in," a Coaching 101 basic. Checking
in first with the other people and other areas of your life before
taking any action step is incredibly helpful and important. It was
a huge wake-up call, but at the same time a huge opportunity to
walk the talk in all areas of my life. This wake-up call by my partner was the impetus for a second, even more powerful, CCC.

*This Cosmic Coach Conversation opened me up
to receive the answers I had previously invited
Spirit/God/Source/the Universe to teach me
about how to love and take care of myself.*

This CCC took place on an otherwise ordinary Saturday. I
had been searching through the classifieds as usual for a part-
time position. I had been doing this for a month or more and
coming up empty. On this particular Saturday, my partner
shared that it still looked as if I were just going through the
motions and that he really couldn't understand why I wouldn't
"just search for a full-time position already."

I really did want him to know I was all-in with him and us,
even if it didn't look that way to him. I also shared that even
though I had resistance to the notion of working just for money or the traditional nine-to-five job, I did share the same views
of feeling confident and being transparent in partnership. I was
committed and willing to do whatever was necessary to helping

him feel more comfortable since, for me, what was more important was his feelings and that these perceived stressors mattered to him.

In that moment, I excused myself and asked him for some time alone to do some self-coaching. My last session had helped me open up to the possibility of even searching for a new "job" at all. But since it also opened the door to essential financial practices, such as a second source of savings, and bringing in more paying coaching clients, my urgency to find that side job had subsided. Meanwhile, his sense of urgency was still just as high, as he was looking at things from the practical view of long-term sustainability. He wasn't yet as confident in my new business endeavor as I now was. But I was also beginning to wonder why my part-time job search wasn't producing the results as quickly as I had anticipated. Signs were pointing to still having an inner energy block around getting the new job.

**Sample CCC Session 2: Let Go and Allow; Release to Receive**
I got comfortable with my trusty pencil, opened my journal, centered myself with some deep breathing, and got fully present with myself. I then checked in with my Cosmic Coach.

Me: "So, I've been looking for a part-time position that would be effortless, fun, and complementary to my new coaching pursuits and spiritual practices, but I am still coming up short. I haven't been the best partner, either, and being an amazing partner to myself and to him is what I want. I also want very much to grow my coaching business and that is why I have stuck to only looking for a part-time position. I am following the path of first asking, "What do I want?" so why is this not working for me now as it usually does? You know, like when I am looking for an apartment and the perfect one suddenly appears or with all of those other effortless *coincidences*? We've discussed it's time for me to start applying for a full-time job, but I can really feel myself resisting that idea. I feel stuck again."

CC: "What are you afraid of?"

Me: "I am afraid that getting a full-time job means I will have to let go of coaching. I finally found something I really love, and I don't want to let it go. But I also really love him, and I don't want to let him go either. I am afraid this could turn into being forced to choose between him and coaching."

CC: "What if the only thing you let go of was the story that having a full-time job would mean that you would lose anything?"

Me: *Silence as I processed this epiphany.* "YES! This makes perfect sense, since it's all just stories and conditioning anyway. Yes! I WANT to let my story go."

As the awareness of this, too, being "just another story" washed over me, the tension I didn't even realize I was carrying in my body released and I could feel a huge softening and re-laxation. Tears streamed from my eyes and down my face as I exhaled and released it all.

Me: "Ahhh yes, there it is. I had no idea I was holding on so tightly to *the HOW.*"

As I let go and felt the release, I was then flooded with exciting thoughts of possibility, like a child getting excited for an adventure.

Me: "What if I can have a job that is full-time, fun, and somehow incorporates my coaching skills? What if the job itself served as a means of bringing me even more coaching clients? What if this new full-time job could be the doorway to building my coaching business effortlessly, like a by-product of just being there? Woohoo, what fun this will be!"

All these thoughts were of the true win-win variety. It felt really good knowing that my partner would get to feel more comfortable with a more traditional, tangible plan of contributing to our financial future. Meanwhile, I knew that whatever job came my way would be effortless from here after this new awareness and subsequent release. I was ready to receive!

I knew this because all my studies up until this point had taught me that "the How" we receive something is not anything we need to worry about or force, as that part was actually up to Spirit/God/Source/the Universe to deliver. I had forgotten what I'd personally taught many people back when I worked at the integrative center: There are multiple *hows*. I forgot that, in reality, there were *hows* that I couldn't even begin to imagine, and that would most likely be even better than I could imagine. "The How" can also be delivered in a perfect synchronicity of events (*coincidences*) that I would not have any control over, so the overall message was that it is better not to leave "the How" up to the limitations of my own mind. Up until this self-coaching session, I had always mentally understood this, but it was finally becoming a part of my inner truth through this experience of Spirit/God/Source/the Universe's life education session.

In the pursuit of co-creating my future, I had already learned how to go inside and reach my inner child to find out what it is that I really want. I had already learned to peel back layers and really get clear on the intention or my *why* under what I want. But, up until then, I thought the magic was just in following "the Want," and it would effortlessly take me where I wanted to be. That so far had been absolutely true for me, but the difference was that up until then I had not experienced any actual resistance to the what that I wanted.

That Saturday was my introduction to what steps to take when there are other parts/personas of me in resistance to what I want. I knew that the next step was to listen closely and validate whatever part of me was in resistance. The new piece I learned was to also find out what *story* was keeping me clinging tightly to the *expectation* of "the How" or in what manner I believed the what that I wanted *should* arrive. Yep, there are always "shoulds" associated with clinging to an expectation!

*Shoulds = rules = conditions = an attachment
to only one way of seeing things. These were
the very things I already learned didn't serve
me if I truly wanted to be free to experience the
fullness of love and joy in this life. I had forgotten
a tightly clenched fist isn't open to receive.*

My own Signature Self-Love Formula was unfolding:

Step 1. Find and follow what I want. (I was already mastering this, and the easiest way was by connecting with my inner little one to help me.)

*Step 2. Let go and allow. Release to receive.*

Tip for releasing/letting go: Find out what I and that previously ignored, resistant inner part of me *both* want. Find a way to align the opposing parts of me on something valuable that they can both get on board with and excited about. Find out what lights them up. For me, this allows the letting go and release of my *how* expectations and leads to more expansion/openness/space to receive. It opens the doors to be surprised by how effortlessly and accessible what I want can be!

Feeling a pure and literal release and then connecting these dots of awareness on that Saturday was both beautiful and awesome. That Saturday will always be the Cosmic Coach Conversation that more personally taught me the magic of *releasing to receive.*

I returned to the living room after the session and sat on the couch next to my partner and opened my laptop to get back to the job search. Within an hour of my switching to the full-time section of the advertisements, I came across a job description that I knew I was A) overqualified for and therefore could B) very likely perform effortlessly and C) do it in an impactful manner they had never seen before, thereby adding tremendous value for them. The position was for a young start-up company that offered a product focused on assisting people in beginning relationships, so it also seemed to easily complement the life and relationship coaching practice I was building.

The question was: Would the company founders be willing to think outside the box and entertain a physician-turned-professional life coach, who in light of the much lower pay would essentially be nearer to volunteering her time and skills toward helping them build their team and serve their clients in a new way? In return, I could gain the reliability factor of having a more traditional position to help my partner relax and be more open to my not-so-traditional, verging on spiritual, coaching endeavor. I could also gain exposure for my coaching business and open the door to a broader network of people. Finally, I could immediately contribute more toward the future home and life that my partner and I were building together. I wrote up a cover letter and applied for the full-time position that very evening of my CCC "Release to Receive" session.

### "Ahhh, I know how to help me!"

Do you remember at the beginning of the book I gave you a forewarning of what to expect while reading this book? That was because following the majority of my transformational coaching sessions, clients share there is typically an initial feeling of excitement or elation from the new light bulb awareness, followed by transient discomfort that may show up hours or many days later. Then the fun coincidental opportunities surface once things within and around you start to shift. Well, here is an example of my own "transient discomfort" that followed when I shined my own coaching light on a previously scary, unseen place within.

That night, following the Cosmic Coach Conversation, the positive momentum and beautiful release from earlier in the day was quickly forgotten when my phone pinged me with a low-balance alert for my checking account. Since educating myself on money had been the topic ever since the previous CCC, and I was reading books on money management, I had intentionally set that alert to remind myself to shift money from savings to checking at regular intervals. I'd learned that the luxury of automatic deposits into my checking account as an employee had actually served as *enabling* of my not being as mindful as I could be of the flow of my own money. With my new practice of being more intentional in my approach to life, and in specific, to money, I was learning how to consciously, instead of blindly, move money around to different accounts depending on my needs and/or wants in the moment.

I was also learning a redefined idea of responsibility. Previously, being the Responsible One meant taking care of everyone else's needs at the expense of my own. My new perspective on responsibility was that I could no longer blame outside sources for my life's situation. Instead, I would take full responsibility for both the desired and the not-so-desired outcomes of my decisions. With responsibility came *the power to change my own situation,* and that was an exciting prospect! In the case of money, I learned I could be mindful and responsible for where, when, and how my money was spent. I got to choose.

But the catch was this. When I invited myself to take a clear look at how I had been approaching responsibility, I would also be gifted by Spirit/God/Source/the Universe with a whole new level of awareness. This meant: A) not only would I be able to select the inner aspects of myself that I wanted to see; but B) I would now also be seeing those shadow aspects I may not have intended to see. Inviting the light to come in allowed me to see what was hidden in the darker, previously unseen, places of my psyche; they would be on full view as a result of the awareness light shining on them. I was now fully seeing all of the fears that came with knowing the truth that, at the end of the day, I was always the only one fully responsible for myself!

And just like that, with the ping from my phone, like a trigger of the subconscious surfacing right on cue, a full-blown panic set in! I was flooded with scary thoughts like: *What if I can't take care of myself? What if I don't get this job, or any job? What if I can't find enough coaching clients and can't successfully build a business? Since most new businesses fail, what if I would be one of those casualties of failed aspirations and dreams? What if I had made the stupidest mistake ever by leaving medicine and a steady reliable six-figure income, and I should have just realized that was my lot in life and just learn to be happy with that? What if chasing my dreams across the country was really me chasing a fairy tale? And now that I was facing reality, what if it was not in the cards for me to have my dreams met, especially this late in life? What if I really was not equipped to take care of my basic needs, and my partner couldn't handle my failure? What if I was doomed to be abandoned again?*

On and on, I flooded myself with these worst-case scenarios and followed them into their rabbit holes of darkness, fear, and panic. My heart was racing, I couldn't breathe, my chest was tight, and I was too scared to even cry. I felt like a deer frozen in headlights. As my partner lay slightly snoring in a deep sleep next to me, I was wide eyed in terror from my fears.

*Ohhh no! What am I going to do?!?* was all I could think to ask myself.

But then the answer came crystal clear, as if so simple and obvious.

CC: "What are you going to do?"

Me: "Ahhh yes, I know what to do. I do know how to help me!"

In the midst of the fears, another, wiser, calmer, clearer part of me simultaneously remembered what to do. That part gently reminded me of what I did know how to do and had already been teaching clients to do, and I just needed to remember. I remembered that I can be here with me and for me; I can give loving attention to myself and meet my own needs, even in the middle of this fearful moment.

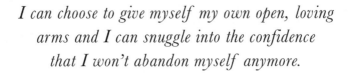

*I can choose to give myself my own open, loving arms and I can snuggle into the confidence that I won't abandon myself anymore.*

As a symbolic gesture of this reminder, while already curled in a fetal position on my side in the bed, with my back toward the rest of the room, I raised the arm I was laying on and wrapped it around the opposite side of me—literally in an attempt to hug my terrified little inner one. The gesture was quick and deliberate, but I still remember it vividly now as if it happened in slow motion. As my right arm wrapped across my chest, I reached toward the opposite shoulder, to pull myself into a self-hug. But then, at the very instant my right hand landed on the back of my left shoulder; I felt the gentle pressure of another hand touching me on my left lower rib area, as if someone invisible standing next to the bed had touched me at the same exact time. Instead of this being terrifying to me, especially since there would not and could not have been anyone else in our apartment touching me, I turned my head and spoke with my thoughts to whomever/whatever it was that touched me, as if that made perfect sense.

Me (the part of me that I was giving the self-hug and was still very much feeling the fear): "No more. I don't want to feel this way anymore. When will this [fear of abandonment] end?"

The One Who Answered: "It already has."

Me: "When? How will I know?"

The One Who Answered: "Tomorrow."

And with that answer, I relaxed and fell asleep in my own arms.

The next morning, I wanted to tell my partner all about what had happened the night before, but there wasn't enough time before he left for work. So, I spent the day focused on all things coaching and felt awe for everything that had happened. *Who was that?* I wondered. *Was it an angel or spirit guide? Was it Mom's ghost? Was there a part of me that doesn't like to remain within my physical body and likes to play at night while I sleep?*

I really didn't need to know who/what it was because in my core I knew that the answers given to me were true. And sure enough, by that afternoon, I received an email from the start-up company saying that they were excited to set up an interview with me for that week. During the interview itself, the company's founder was clearly so pleasantly surprised at what a perfect win-win fit hiring me would be that he said, "Wow, Lana. It's like you just dropped out of the sky as an answer to what we were looking for."

I told him I agreed it was a perfect fit, while on the inside I could hear little Lou giggling, "If he only knew!" Lou and I both knew, and now without any residual doubt, that none of these *coincidences* were ever coincidental.

# CHAPTER 17

# *Treasure Found*

What was the take-home message that Lou (and that clear knowing voice) taught me?

*That this majestic, lovable inner child treasure
IS me! That she was me then and now. She's
not some lost version of me that got left behind!
She's always been me. I just stopped being her!*

She's my treasure found, and I am so in love!

Remember my personal Signature Self-Love Formula that was unfolding?

Step 1. Find and follow what I want.

Step 2. Let go and allow. Release to receive.

Well, here's step 3.

## Step 3. If it lights me up, it's meant for me!

My most exciting epiphany was realizing for myself that Spirit/ God/Source/the Universe is already abundant . . . unconditional . . . and without limits. There's an endless source of love and joy to be found! If I focus on what lights me up or what makes my heart smile and then let that fill me up, I'm flooded with love and joy that I in turn want to radiate out to the world. What lights me up essentially flows to and then from me. In other words, when I get inspired, I in turn inspire others and their inspiration inspires me even more...and so on. When I love myself and others unconditionally, I am loved unconditionally and so are they. I find now that when I say "I want X" simply because it lights me up, then X *coincidentally* finds its way to me.

I'm sure the yogis, lightworkers, or energy readers out there surely can explain this better than I can, but while writing this book, I found an article by intuitive physician Laura Koniver, M.D. She perfectly describes what I've been attempting to share with you, except she put it in terms of chakras. Regarding the second chakra, she writes: "The sacral chakra is where your inner child lives. Your inner child and your soul have no end to creative ideas, an abundance of energy, and joy and freedom in expressing your unique gifts."[1] I can attest there certainly was a creative flow while writing this book, and I hope to continue to embrace Lou's reminder to choose to see life's magic through the eyes of a child.

It also goes without question that loving and listening to my inner child led me to experience a full, open heart! Again quoting

Dr. Koniver, "*I am guided, I am not alone,* is the heart chakra's message."[2] This was exactly the message I was led to find! Lou (and that clear, knowing voice) showed me how lovable and how NOT alone I really am. And I wish the same discovery for you!

My heart now is more often than not wide open and continues to experience that beautiful, warm alchemy. It's been a daily (and sometimes not easy) practice for me to intentionally choose love first, and the journey has been so worth it! I'm certainly not saying that I am always successful at being mindfully present, but each discomfort, each challenge, becomes a reminder to return to this moment, to be present with myself and show ME-Love. (Hugging myself when necessary, too.) I remember to just be; be in connection with Spirit, with the Essence of all things. I'm reminded it is all just the illusion of stories and conditioning anyway, and then I am able to see there's so much to love.

As a parting gesture, little Lou would like to invite you to begin a baby step toward creating your own Signature Self-Love Formula with this fun first-step exercise.

1. Grab something to write with and an empty journal. I'm "old school" so I still love writing with paper and pencil. For this, you can substitute your laptop or smartphone. Open a blank document or start a new text message to yourself.

2. Find a comfortable, peaceful place where you won't be interrupted for at least ten minutes.

3. Write down (or text yourself) the following two questions to ask your own inner little one. Yes, you are literally writing down these questions to ask yourself!

- What kinds of things excite you, energize you, or fill you up?
- What do you deeply want to experience and how can I (meaning you) help make that happen?

4. Wait for the answers and write down (or text yourself) ANY answers that come to you.

5. If the only thing that comes to you is a list of reasons why you *can't* have or experience these things, then we invite you to ponder this additional question:

*What if the only thing missing is for you to love YOU without conditions?*

# PART FOUR

## *diamonds and pearls*

# CHAPTER 18

# *Gem Lessons*

I'm still in awe of how life unfolds when we relax and go with it. I am still in awe of how all the symptoms of what I used to define as suffering were really *invitations* to take a closer look. These invitations were my Gem Lessons—all of those diamonds and pearls. And little Lou had been right there waiting for me to stop abandoning her and accept the invitation to be free to live a more loving, abundant, joyous life.

I have enjoyed how much playful fun it is to see the world through Lou's eyes first, and then remembering that I am her, has brought me. In even the smallest moments, Lou loves to play with the little one inside my creative-friend-turned-partner (and now husband). My willingness to finally listen to Lou and experience the magical wonder that came with exploring her viewpoint is what prompted me to share her story with the "little one" in you. Recalling what Toni Morrison said, *"If there's a book that you want to read but it hasn't been written yet, then you must write it,*[1] I knew I'd one day allow Lou to help me write. Having shared her journey with you in a raw and transparent way, my hope is that it spoke to you and helped you see what's possible for you.

Anytime you are in need of a quick, inspirational reminder of the gems that are the lessons I learned, please come back to this section of the book. It is dedicated to you. Please read the following summaries of the **DIAMONDS** and **PEARLS**. Along with these gems, you'll find corresponding coaching questions for you and your inner little one to contemplate. Play with the awareness that comes from just one gem lesson at a time. With increased awareness comes the ability to see with more clarity. Awareness opens a treasure chest of previously unseen exciting possibilities and opportunities. Enjoy!

# GEM LESSON 1

## Don't Earn Your Worth, Own Your Worth

*We are worthy, majestic, and absolutely lovable, no matter what anyone (including our own inner critic) tries to tell us!*

**Page xiii.** Would I live my life differently if I knew mistakes and failures, judgments, and criticisms didn't actually matter?

- ♦ YES, YES, and even more YES! How about you?

**Page 14.** On a deeper level, after the night Mom died, I bought into the belief that I wasn't worthy of being taken care of, cherished, or nurtured.

- Here's an invitation for your inner little one to pretend that you just discovered you are a royal heiress/heir. Sit for a moment and experience how that would feel.

- How would you spend your time if you actually believed your dreams were possible?

**Page 15.** For most families, the unspoken rules let a child know: "You will be considered a good kid and I will give you love, but only under these conditions."

- What unspoken family rules are you still following that may no longer be serving you?

- In what areas of your life might you be trying to earn love instead of knowing you are worthy of it without having to do anything?

**Page 47.** Seeing my value only as it related to other people's expectations of me had become my way of life, but I couldn't yet see at what cost.

- What are your criteria for feeling valuable, deserving, or worthy of happiness?

**Page 89.** My focus was still completely outside myself. I was always looking for external validation to give me what may as well have been "approval" for my very existence. My value was still only what others said it was.

♦ How much do you believe you are completely lovable, with nothing missing, just as you are?

# GEM LESSON 2

## Never Underestimate the Wisdom and Purity of a Child

*My wise, majestic, lovable inner little Lou led me home. As a child, my heart was wide open. My eyes saw wonder and magic in everything. Listening to that inner little one, loving that little one, and becoming that little one again were my keys to unlock all my locked doors, and my connection back to Spirit/God/Source/the Universe.*

**Page 5.** I've just learned to listen to myself better.

♦ Where or when have you ignored your own inner voice or have not been listening to yourself?

**Page 19.** I never thought of doing anything else because my decisions were not coming from the place of knowing what I really wanted to do or what I felt passionate about.

♦ Ask your inner little one, what would light you up and make you excited to wake up each morning?

♦ What is stopping you from doing those things every day?

♦ What is one thing you can choose to do today just because you would love to?

# GEM LESSON 3

## This One Life Is Ours, but How Easily We Forget Ourselves

*There are endless sneaky ways we turn our backs on ourselves and abandon ourselves each day. Meanwhile, we're right here waiting for us to remember and get back to really experiencing the gift that is our life!*

**Page 16.** My underlying motive was to do whatever was necessary to avoid a similar abandonment by Dad.

- ◆ How often do you ask yourself, *Why am I really doing the things I find myself doing every day?*
- ◆ What fears might be hidden motives for you?
- ◆ What are the benefits you receive when allowing fear to be your true decision maker?

**Page 20.** Blind unquestioning, going through the motions, making choices from a place of seeking approval, and avoiding abandonment had become my MO.

- ◆ Where in your life, even if it seems noble or honorable, could you be on autopilot or just going through the motions?
- ◆ How does the approval of others factor into your thoughts, actions, decisions?

**Page 24.** Over and over, I continued to abandon myself as I took on more of these identities.

- How would your life or relationships change if you showed up authentically?
- What if the "you" at home or the "you" with your friends showed up to your workplace?
- Which version of "you" are you the most comfortable showing to the world?
- Which version of you do you WANT to be you all day?

**Page 28.** Meanwhile, somewhere in a dark corner inside me, Lou curled up and cried from the pain of abandonment again.

- At the end of your life, what would the future you say to the little one inside of you when he/she tries to explain why you never got around to experiencing the things you promised him/her as a child?

**Page 28.** Little by little, one small choice followed by another, everything that Lou was happy doing disappeared.

- How many times in the day do you make a choice for the pure purpose of really making yourself smile and feel happy?
- How willing are you to stop making excuses and start making yourself happier today?

**Page 29.** I was going through the necessary motions to earn praise, attention, and approval, get scholarships, and have my basic needs met, but it was always at the cost of turning my back on Lou and my authenticity.

- What areas of life are you settling for less than what you really want?
- What tiny, easy, effortless thing can you commit to doing every day that would at least point you in the direction of what you really want?

**Page 173.** When I remember to simply follow my heart's desire, or let love lead, I am free to co-create any life I wish to experience. The choice is mine.

- What has your inner little one been nudging you to remember to do?
- What would you say if someone tells you that you have something to offer the world?

# GEM LESSON 4

## Give the Gift of Presence

*When we give our full attention and can be truly present, it can feel as if time stops; and in that space, we can remember what truly matters. For me now, the ultimate gift in life is simply being present for the experience of it. I want to be here. I want to live life to its fullest and have the capacity to experience as much love, joy, and magic as possible. Presence, in its many forms (for example, stillness, intimacy, mindfulness, meditation, yoga), whether it be with myself and my partner or with*

*animals and nature, becomes my gateway for communion with*
*Spirit/God/Source/the Universe.*

*"What you perceive as precious is not time but the one point that*
*is out of time: the Now. That is precious indeed. The more you are*
*focused on time—past and future—the more you miss the Now,*
*the most precious thing there is."²*
—*Eckhart Tolle*

**Page 27.** I deeply craved even the tiniest moments of attention from someone who loved me, and this reinforced me in doing whatever I needed to get more of them.

◆ What does genuine loving attention actually feel like?

**Page 78.** In hindsight, overextending myself gave me a convenient excuse to be too busy to really enjoy life or to work on improving the quality of my relationships.

◆ Where are you making excuses for being present enough to fully experience your life?

**Page 93.** All my focus was on him and very little of my focus was on me.

◆ Where might you be giving away your power or your energy that could be used elsewhere to better serve you and your dreams?

◆ What area of your life would LOVE your attention?

**Page 109.** Living on autopilot and not stopping long enough to notice.

- What activities in your day, even if honorable, might be a disguised distraction from being present with yourself?

- If you could give yourself a long-overdue date night (or date day) with yourself, what would that look like?

**Page 183.** Inviting the gifts of loving people and resources into your current awareness begins with dialing into the experience of your own loving attention.

- What percentage of the day are you "dialed in" to your own experience? In other words, how often are you lost in thought or in your work and forget your surroundings; or don't notice how you feel...or forget yourself?

- How would your day change if you took the time to stop, check in, and ask yourself: *How am I doing, how do I feel, what do I need in this moment?*

**Page 187.** Unknown to me, all of those years I had been suffering from the ailment that life begins at some elusive "One Day."

- What benefits, if any, might come from prioritizing this moment (now), instead of always waiting for "one day"?

- Cool! What do you WANT to prioritize first?

# GEM LESSON 5

## Experiencing the Magic of Presence Began with the Practice of Intentionally Focusing Attention

*The ability to retrain our brains and choose where we want to place our focus improves with practice. The more we focus in one area, the more we "filter out" certain things and "filter in" other things that better support our focus. The practice of intentionally focusing our attention (for example, with meditation or mindfulness) increases our capacity to simultaneously be aware of multiple possibilities and consciously choose our actions instead of following the usual autopilot conditioned reactions.*

*"Where attention goes, neural firing flows, and neural connection grows."*[3]
—*Daniel J Siegel, M.D*

**Page 32.** Unfortunately, somehow Lou selectively forgot other songs with more inspiring vibes to which she could have just as easily chosen to cling.

- How able are you to walk into any situation and then stop and choose to see it differently with a fresh pair of eyes and without the limitations of your previous focus?
- Pick one phrase you are known to say a lot. If you are not sure, ask your friends/family. What more powerful, inspiring, expansive, or joyful phrase would you prefer to be known for saying?

**Page 44.** Intense focus and only giving attention to form, breath, and what was right in front of me proved to be a skill Lou taught me that I could use to my advantage in the future.

- ♦ What practices have you found that work to keep your brain from running down the rabbit hole of repetitive fearful thoughts or unproductive reactivity?

- ♦ If none have worked for you, here is a list of some practices I've done over the years that I have enjoyed and found helpful: Stillness. Meditation. Mindfulness. Drawing (or anything creative). Dancing. Visualization. Yoga. Tibetan Singing Bowls (or any music that draws you in to focus on each note). Dr Dan Seigel's Wheel of Awareness guided meditation. Exercising "in the zone."

# GEM LESSON 6

## There Are Some Things We Still Learn the Hard Way

*I just think of it now as squeezing a diamond from carbon. I also remember to have compassion when I'm reminded there is a part of me that must believe these repetitive self-sabotaging patterns are actually for my own good or for some secondary gain.*

*"Nothing ever goes away until it has taught us what we need to know."*[4]
—*Pema Chodron*

**Page 30.** I'm sure it is no surprise to you that in my efforts to run away from what I didn't want, I *coincidentally* ran right smack into exactly that.

- ◆ Where in your life have you noticed that no matter what you do or how hard you try, you keep ending up in the same frustrating situation?
- ◆ What if that same frustrating repeating pattern could be seen as a clue on a treasure hunt?

**Page 30.** Why else would anyone agree to ignore their dreams and forgo their needs, and lose so many years of her life, if there wasn't some form of secondary gain in so doing?

- ◆ Secondary gain can come in many forms. Consider an area of your life that you really want to change. Now ask yourself:
  - What am I gaining by not changing it?
  - What am I afraid I'd lose if I do change it?

**Page 34.** In this vast universe, she could be hopeful that the Bible verse that read "All things [in the Universe] work together for good" (Romans 8:28) was true.

- ◆ What "bad" things in your life ended up exactly the best thing ever?
- ◆ If you can't come up with anything on your own, ask three friends that same question.

**Page 47.** Life has a way of getting our attention when we are ignoring our own inner voice of wisdom.

♦ What comes up for you when you read the following words? *Sometimes what seems super horrible (like losing a job or a relationship's end) is just the gift we need to stop our sleepwalking and be jolted awake.*

**Page 110.** One such lesson was that if I wanted a change to happen, I had to make a change.

♦ If you didn't have to worry about how, which repeating pattern would you commit to ending today?

# GEM LESSON 7

## Honor All Your Feelings

*There was so much to learn from my neglected, suppressed feelings. When I finally stopped running away and stopped trying to protect myself from the very real deep pain of feeling abandoned and unworthy, my entire life changed to amazing. Something as simple as validating (what I now call honoring) the little girl inside of me who just needed me to love her through that pain was all that was required to shift toward true freedom and experiencing bigger, deeper love than I could have imagined. Now I know that on the other side of feeling is healing!*

**Page 40.** There was certainly plenty of competitive, aggressive, and productive (masculine) energy in our home, but very little energy that was associated with peace, stillness, and creative (feminine) flow.

- How would you describe the difference between "driven" and "inspired action"?
- What does peace feel like?

**Page 100.** I was finally feeling it all with nowhere else to run, no identity to escape into.

- What would you need to feel at peace with a potential unforeseen outcome?
- In what ways might your life heal or expand if you allowed yourself to feel more?

**Page 100.** The truth was that I spent my life trying to prevent feeling this very pain, the pain that was born That Night I watched Mom turn her back on me and walk away from our lives forever.

- Where in your body do you feel anger, sadness, or anxiety?
- What benefit might there be to allowing yourself to feel all of your feelings, even the uncomfortable ones?
- If your heart could talk, what message has it been trying to give you?

**Page 122.** But as I applied the new inward-looking techniques I'd been learning, my body revealed multiple hidden painful and/or numb areas that still desperately needed my attention.

- What benefit can you see in taking the advice from this anonymous quote? *"Listen to your body when it whispers, and you won't have to hear it scream."*
  —Unknown

# GEM LESSON 8

### With Questions Come Answers

*The most powerful tools in a coach's toolbox are her intuitive questions. When we are living on autopilot, sleepwalking, and living from our conditioned thinking and patterns, we can't possibly be aware of what we don't know. We can't know there may be so much more than our current limiting view has the ability to fathom. When we are open to questioning and open to hearing the answers, the answers follow and our awareness expands.*

**Page 53.** Instead of questioning, I simply assumed all of those years that all of the rules and conditions expected of me were really in my best interest.

- ◆ What unquestioned rules are you still following that may not be in your best interest?

**Page 53.** I had been living with the simple childlike logic of following rules = needs met. I never stopped to get curious and ask questions like: What and whose needs are these rules really meeting? How exactly are they meeting mine? Could there be other means of meeting my needs that I would actually enjoy?

- ◆ Your turn: Could there be other means of meeting your needs that you would enjoy more than the current life rules you are following?

**Page 76.** Do we really stand a chance of seeing clearly when our unexplored hidden deeper unmet needs are leading the way?

- ♦ What top two questions would you ask your future self if you knew the answers would ensure your future happiness?

**Page 177.** If it were possible that you repeatedly felt infuriated as a child by something very similar, what name could you give that childhood identity that would be telling me this same story?

- ♦ What Disney character (archetype) would best tell your childhood story? (For example, little Lou's story of "*I always have to do extra chores and work, while my sister gets to have fun*" often made her sound like Cinderella to me.)
- ♦ What character could you create for yourself that feels better or more inspiring to you?

**Page 195.** This Cosmic Coach Conversation opened me up to receive the answers I had previously invited Spirit/God/Source/ the Universe to teach me about how to love and take care of myself.

- ♦ How open are you to hear suggestions that could improve your current life situation?
- ♦ What if you really believed it could be as simple as "ask and you shall receive"?

# GEM LESSON 9

## Presence Matters

*Without quieting my mind and being fully present and still, I would not have been able to hear little Lou. I am by no means an expert in this spiritual practice, as I am still growing and learning, but what I can say for sure is that my answers always came when I first asked the question and then intentionally became still and present. The more I practiced presence, the more the previously hidden gems came into view.*

**Page 35.** The voice was ever so small, but always clear and definitive.

- ♦ How open are you to allowing Spirit/God/Source/the Universe, your spirit guides, and/or your higher self to speak to you?
- ♦ What is your clear sign that life supports you?

# GEM LESSON 10

## All Relationships Matter

*How we relate to ourselves is often reflected back at us in our external relationships, whether it be family or partners or colleagues or even pets.*

**Page 53.** It was the first glimpse of how good it could feel to put my own well-being and self-care first. But yet it still required someone outside of me, this time the head coach, to give me permission and make it so.

- If you are not feel completely cared for and fulfilled, what are you waiting for?
- What one change can you make today toward taking better care of yourself?

**Page 75.** How people relate to animals will tell you a lot about how they relate to themselves and how they show up in relationships.

- If your most recent interactions with your pet (or your best friend or your partner or your child) were filmed without your knowledge, what would someone watching that clip learn about you?

**Page 87.** It was fascinating to feel what it was like to have another being attuned to me, sensing my energy, and interested in looking out for me this time.

- In whose company do you feel safe enough to just be alive and fully relaxed?
- How much does the company you keep reflect how you really want to be treated?
- Observe your pet for a day or take time out to watch animals in nature for an hour. What did you learn from what you observed?

# GEM LESSON 11

## Remember, It's All Just Stories and Conditioning

*As children, when we tried to navigate our earliest environments, we often internalized the spoken and unspoken messages, even if those messages didn't serve us. But under all of those self-defeating critical stories and conditioning, we are part of the same Essence in everything. We can choose to make that what matters.*

**Page 53.** I could only have the mindset/perspective/view from where I was at that time, with my combined lifetime of experiences and conditioning up until that point.

◆ Think of the journey of a seed to sapling to tree or of a caterpillar to chrysalis to butterfly. If it were true that each stage of our journey can bring the opportunity for a new perspective, what possibilities can you now imagine lie ahead of you that you could not have known from your current view?

**Page 101.** These were the explanations I subconsciously created at seven years old to make sense of my painful world and were the very beliefs that led me to a life of neglecting, abusing, and abandoning myself in return.

◆ When was the last time you did a spring cleaning of your long-held critical beliefs about yourself that you've carried with you this far into adulthood?

**Page 101.** With that question, and as a glimpse of the slightest compassion for my mother's predicament entered my awareness, something else awakened in me to see that all of this is a choice.

- Even if you already consider yourself to be full of compassion, what additional opportunities could come from being even *more* compassionate?
- What opportunities might be waiting for you if finally dropped your current story that has kept you behind a wall of settling for just OK?
- How willing are you to open up and allow love to lead?

**Page 126.** I wanted to keep unlearning the patterns of self-abandonment and neglect that I had mastered, and I wanted to continue learning more and more about co-creating with Spirit/God/Source/the Universe and thriving in a beautiful new life without fear.

- If there is something inside telling you the time to make a significant change in your life is now, what would help you feel good and on board with the change?
- Whether you choose to play a part in making a change or not, it is always up to you how you will experience change.
    - Will you resist change and suffer as it happens anyway?
    - Will you actively participate by choosing to embrace change and be part of writing your own story?
    - What benefits could there be in letting go, sitting back, and watching in awe as changes unfold in front of you?

♦ When you look at the lives of people you admire, what practical tips can you learn from their clear examples of thriving—instead of just surviving—through change?

**Page 157.** This truth became crystal clear: We are all doing the best that we can with the conditioning we have and the limited awareness we have access to in any moment.

♦ We don't know what we don't know, until we finally become aware of it. Take a deep breath and bring into your awareness any "conditioned" idea you may want to examine. Are there opinions or judgments that were taught to you as a child that may not really be authentic for you anymore?

♦ What behaviors did your family/culture/society praise as "good" or condemn as "bad"? Are those behaviors always "good" or "bad" in every situation?

♦ Play a game with me and ask yourself this question: *If I could erase the stories I've been carrying about the past, what new story could I choose to tell that would positively shape my future?*

**Page 165.** Meanwhile, I, a full-grown adult, hadn't even been conscious of the fact I was still listening to this childhood creation!

♦ How often is each statement below true for you?
    - I am consciously choosing to see life through the playful eyes of a visionary child.
    - I am unconsciously trying to prevent the pervasive childhood fears of losing approval for not

being accomplished enough/beautiful, fashion-able, or cool enough/smart enough.

**Page 199.** Shoulds = rules = conditions = attachment to only one way of seeing things. These were the very things I already learned didn't serve me if I truly wanted to be free to experience the fullness of love and joy in this life. I had forgotten a tightly clenched fist isn't open to receive.

♦ The most common "clenched fist" pattern I've witnessed in myself was my unflinching expectation that a certain way (how) to receive what I wanted was also the *right* way to receive it. But I later learned that gripping so tightly to this *right* way was usually what was precisely preventing me from receiving. I learned there were actually multiple other ways it could have come to me that I hadn't yet thought of. What "clenched fist" pattern is/was true for you?

♦ What expectation can you experiment loosening your grip on, even if only as a game, to try and see what comes from letting go?

# GEM LESSON 12

## Perspective Matters

*We can choose the view or perspective that sees our value. We can choose to release the stories and see love.*

**Page 68.** As it is with 20-20 hindsight, there were gifts right in front of us that we couldn't see.

- ♦ I invite you to close your eyes and imagine there's a gift you've been anticipating for years and it is now sitting right outside of your front door. With your eyes still closed and before you open that door, do a quick check-in with the rest of your life.
- ♦ What is that gift to yourself you've been waiting for?
- ♦ What would need to happen to ensure you are ready to receive that gift right now?
- ♦ What would change in your life once the gift is fully received?

**Page 146.** At the heart of it all, the perspective was always what mattered.

- ♦ Picture yourself standing across the street from a man and a woman in the park. The man's back is to you and the woman is seated in front of him on a park bench, so his back is obstructing the view of her face.

  You can see her arms are folded across her body and she is slumped forward. His arms are raised overhead and he's waving them around with big gestures. You can hear the volume of his voice is loud, and from your view he appears to be shouting down at the woman. Your initial deduction from your view is that he must be verbally abusing this woman and she is slumped forward with folding arms from humiliation.

But just as you start to judge this man for being a complete asshole, you walk forward a few steps. From this new view you can see the woman is indeed leaning forward but her arms are folded across her stomach because she is belly laughing at him while he acts out a scene from a comedy.

♦ How much space do you allow for alternative perspectives before you judge a situation, judge others, or judge yourself?

**Page 153.** I loved the premise of Core Energy Coaching™ that with each conscious choice, we free ourselves from the confines of limited perspectives and gain access to experiencing whatever amazing life we want!

♦ If you really believed you were able to experience so much more in this lifetime, what would you want to experience first?

**Page 160.** How open am I to the possibility that we all have a choice either to keep the core beliefs that were indeed necessary once in the past or to choose new ones that may better serve us now in the present?

♦ Picture someone you currently look up to for experiencing things in this life that you only wish you could. What core beliefs might they be choosing to follow that you aren't?

**Page 172.** It became crystal clear to me that when I do these things I become IMPRISONED by the RULES and CONDITIONS associated with my perceptions.

♦ What areas have you imprisoned yourself or seen someone else imprison themselves in an imaginary cage of your/their own making (even if that cage is beautifully decorated or feels completely necessary)?

**Page 145.** Together we were learning that perspective matters. Shifting perspective allows us to see more possibilities and previously hidden opportunities.

♦ Even someone who seemingly has everything knows there are things they believe are out of their reach. For example, someone with wealth may believe they'll never find a partner who sees, accepts, and loves them for who they are instead of for what they have or how much they've accomplished.

♦ What hidden or buried longing have you given up on that may just benefit from a fresh or shifted perspective?

# GEM LESSON 13

## Conscious Inspired Action Feels Effortless

*When we do what inspires us, when we are purposefully productive, and when we do what brings us joy, the doing feels effortless. "Growing pains" become "light bulb moments of expansion." Enjoyable, buildable, effortless practice is now my preferred method for work and growth. When we love what we do and have the added knowledge that we are contributing to life with our unique experiences, skill sets, and gifts, there no longer exists a separation of work and life. We are just being the most authentic version of ourselves, which in itself is our contribution. My best work now feels natural and comes from just being me.*

**Page 51.** The exercise was tailored around how I felt while doing it.

♦ If we aren't feeling good while we work, we have at least three options. Keep feeling poorly and make the best of it. Find a way to change how you feel at work. Only do work that feels good.

♦ Which option resonates with you as the option you'd prefer?

♦ Close your eyes and recall the happiest or most joyful moment in your life. How long are you able to bask in the memory and breathe that moment in as if it is happening now?

**Page 52**. This new approach to training made the progress feel effortless.

As Tony Robbins says: "Remember, the little things aren't little —they're everything…And it is in making these 2 mm shifts now that you can achieve the most astounding results tomorrow."[5] So, even the smallest shift in a new direction leads to a completely new place when you follow that trajectory out for the distance.

♦ What simple, basic step that is aligned with your vision can you take today?

♦ What additional step can you add tomorrow?

**Page 143.** What do I enjoy doing almost tirelessly, because the work inspires me at my core?

- Same question: What do you enjoy doing without tiring because the work inspires you at your core?

- If you are already doing that inspired work, how does the rest of your life feel in comparison?

- Does your whole life feel just as inspiring and effortless, and if not, what needs to shift to make it so?

- When was the last time you felt so aligned with your purpose that life unfolded perfectly for you with convenient coincidences and seemingly no effort on your part?

**Page 157.** The experiences of my life had been helping me hone and develop skills I could one day use to help other people.

- What life experiences have you been telling yourself were bad draws of the cards or unfortunate setbacks that could actually have been the perfect preparation for you to be of enormous impact?

- How willing are you to see yourself as a bright lighthouse for those who are still tossed around in dark seas of their lives by similar pounding waves?

**Page 159.** In summary, my "all too real" life education, with its twists, turns, heartbreaks, and layering of knowledge would serve me very well as a coach.

- In a coaching session with one of my clients, she opened up enough space in herself to see the current stage of her life was really what she coined as her "Higher Purpose Training Ground."

♦ What will you be calling the degree you'll receive once you graduate from this chapter of *Your Life's Education?*

**Page 190.** Meeting needs can be done effortlessly and in ways that are enjoyable.

♦ What comes up for you as I ask you to revisit the current paradigm of "hard work must *feel* hard too"?

♦ What areas has life already helped you become a master of something that you genuinely enjoy as well?

♦ If you have trouble seeing your own mastery, consider this tiny example. I was shocked to learn that for some people preparing a holiday family dinner is viewed as hard work and stressful. From that view, they can stress themselves out in the days leading up to the holiday, then isolate themselves with all of the prepping and cooking, and as a result, end up missing out on a fun time visiting with loved ones. Thanks to my personal life experience as a "parentified child," meal prep comes effortlessly to me and I had actually been using my skills in the kitchen to my advantage. I had no idea that not everyone intentionally invited family over early like I do to be with them in the kitchen while I cook and listen to them talk. I use the many hours it takes to prepare a holiday meal as an opportunity to experience quality time talking, singing, laughing, and listening to music with loved ones. You, too, may already be a master in areas of your life that you've taken for granted.

# GEM LESSON 14

## Consider That Coincidences May Not Be All That Coincidental!

*Things coincidentally fell into place when I was not just willing to but **wanting** to love myself and prioritize what brought me joy. I learned self-validation, as defined by really honoring, understanding, and seeing life through the eyes of the little one inside of me. This was followed by wanting to see that little one in me light up and making sure to prioritize doing those things. It felt like the coincidences came flooding in after that as a nod of support for my new self-love efforts.*

**Page 125.** I was free to make my own decisions and I could put myself as a priority.

- ♦ What percentage of your day do you prioritize you?
- ♦ What benefits have you and those around you experienced whenever you have actually prioritized yourself?

**Page 129.** It was another amazing reinforcement of my own ability to give loving attention to myself.

- ♦ As children, we were not capable of meeting all of our needs and did need to look outside of ourselves. As capable adults, what excuses are we making for not giving ourselves all of the love and attention we want and need?

**Page 136.** She just wanted permission to play.

- ♦ What is your inner little one waiting for permission to do, to have, to experience in this lifetime?
- ♦ How ready are you to live a full life?

**Page 149.** What do I want my future to look like?

- ♦ Take a moment and picture your life in ten years as if nothing has changed and you haven't followed through on any of the things you keep promising to do for yourself.
- ♦ How do you feel in that future?
- ♦ What do you want that future to look and feel like instead?

**Page 178.** Awareness arises that these childhood creations are simply using this current uncomfortable situation in your life as an opportunity to get your attention and speak to you.

- ♦ If you could give the ignored, abandoned, stifled parts of yourself a safe, confidential space of nonjudgment to finally speak up and express themselves, what would those parts of you say?

# GEM LESSON 15

## Make It Simple

*We love to complicate everything!*

**Page 115.** I was experiencing positive growth opportunities simply from intentionally placing myself in an environment that was aligned with who I wanted to become.

- Something as simple as looking around your home or your workspace can help you better align with the vision of you loving yourself or having your dream life.
- What tiny change can you make in your environment that would support your vision?

**Page 200.** Let go and allow. Release to receive.

- What are you fearful of letting go in order to receive what you really want?

**Page 204.** I can choose to give myself my own open, loving arms and I can snuggle into the confidence that I won't abandon myself anymore.

- What is your signature practice for letting yourself know you are loved, lovable, and that you will always be there for you?

# GEM LESSON 16

## Abundance Comes from an Unconditional, Limitless Source

*When I finally looked around, I could see there is abundance everywhere: stars in the universe, blades of grass, grains of sand, regenerating cells in our bodies, recycling water from oceans to clouds to rain to ice on mountaintops to streams and rivers, and the energy connecting all of it. Who am I to put restrictions on Spirit, on life, on possibilities, on love?*

**Page 58.** From a place of fullness, we are always better equipped to take care of others.

♦ Many of us have all been there: giving from empty. But what does it really feel like to give from a full or overflowing cup?

♦ What if we could make that the new normal for giving?

**Page 61.** Living with debt as a way of life, instead of being taught to live from fullness and abundance and then giving from the overflow, was one of the many "house rules" I would forget to question as the Doctor.

♦ My story used to be, "I don't have enough money to save. I have to pay off all of this debt first!" I finally learned to flip the script and prioritized myself along with paying any dues. What script is it about time you flipped in your favor?

**Page 155.** Unconditional love is love without conditions.

+ The illusion is that love has limits. If we love and give to others, we somehow fear we might not have enough left to give to ourselves, too. But real love doesn't ration, it doesn't make you earn it, it is there in abundance for you always. How might your life change if you could believe this?

+ What if all that is missing is for you to love YOU without limits or conditions?

**Page 168.** I am full of light and love. I have an opportunity to fulfill a purpose: to let my light shine as a gift to others to help them see their own.

+ How aware are you of your own light?

+ What would it take to see yourself as a shiny gem of immense intrinsic value?

**Page 171.** I was opening up more and more space for compassion and for the capacity to love bigger than I could imagine.

+ Do you have any feelings of resistance when you think of receiving any of these from someone:
  o Sympathy?
  o Acknowledgment?
  o Validation?
  o Forgiveness?
  o Empathy?
  o Compassion?
  o Acceptance?

- If so, why?
- If not, how consistently do you give these to yourself?

**Page 183.** It's like inviting Spirit/God/Source/the Universe and those around you to give you exactly what you want, by actually wanting it enough to be willing to give it to yourself.

- If it's true that we are always teaching others by our own example, what are you teaching others about how you want to be treated, cared for, or loved?

**Page 207.** That this majestic, lovable inner child treasure IS me! That she was me then and now. She's not some lost version of me that got left behind! She's always been me. I just stopped being her!

- Who do you know that always seems to shine like a brightly polished diamond?
- Would more joy, more love, or more magical influence be reasons enough to free yourself to shine?

# AN INVITATION TO
# LOOK WITH ME™

I'd love to support you on your journey to full-on unconditional love for yourself and assist you in creating a vision for a life full of joy. Revealing your authentic self and expressing your gifts is one of the best ways to love yourself and let your light shine.

Can you see the treasure that is you? I can!

Come look with me through a series of one-on-one personal coaching sessions, group coaching, and upcoming Treasure Found retreats. Find details on my website: www.lookwithme-coaching.com.

I'd also love to hear about your own Treasure Found self-love story! Please find me on Instagram @lookwithmecoach.

Let's share using any or all of these hashtags:

#treasurefound

#somuchtolove

#lookwithme

#gemlessons

# showMElove

#signatureselfloveformula

#freetoshine

# NOTES

## Chapter 4 – The Workhorse (aka the Student-Athlete)

1 Cork Gaines and Mark Nudelman, "The average college football team makes more money than the next 35 college sports combined," *Business Insider*, October 5, 2017, https://www.businessinsider.com/college-sports-football-revenue-2017-10.

2 Cork Gaines, "Chart Shows How Little of College Sports Revenues Goes to the Athletes," *Business Insider*, September 25, 2014, https://www.businessinsider.com/college-sports-revenue-athlete-scholarships-2014-9.

## Chapter 5 – The Doctor

1 Pauline Anderson, "Doctors' Suicide Rate Highest of Any Profession," WebMD.com, May 8, 2018, https://www.webmd.com/mental-health/news/20180508/doctors-suicide-rate-highest-of-any-profession#1.

## Chapter 8 – Nowhere Else to Run (aka at Rock Bottom)

1 Harville Hendrix, Ph.D. and Helen Hunt, Ph.D., "What is Imago Relationship Therapy," harvilleandhelen.com (accessed April 13, 2019), https://harvilleandhelen.com/initiatives/what-is-imago/.

## Chapter 10 – Learning That Attention Matters

1 Wikipedia, "Mindfulness" (accessed April 13, 2019), https://en.wikipedia.org/wiki/Mindfulness.

2 "101 Best Louise Hay Affirmations of All Time," LouiseHay.com (accessed April 13, 2019), https://www.louisehay.com/101-best-louise-hay-positive-affirmations.

**Chapter 13 – Free to Follow My Heart**

1   "Core Competencies," International Coach Federation (accessed April 13, 2019), https://coachfederation.org/core-competencies.

**Chapter 14 – Thank You, iPEC**

1   "Discover Next-Level Coaching Methods to Dig Deeper," ipeccoaching.com (accessed April 13, 2019), https://www.ipeccoaching.com/core-energy-coaching?hsCtaTracking=06278b6b-c9f8-43cd-84b7-a6165930e6ef%7Cc3af5b00-1e38-419f-87de-2c8a77fe9941.

2   Jalal ad-Din Rumi, http://www.bbc.co.uk/worldservice/learningenglish/movingwords/quotefeature/rumi.shtml; OR *A Course in Miracles* (page 338 chapter 16 IV:6).

3   M.D. Lieberman, et al., "Putting Feelings into Words: Affect Labeling Disrupts Amygdala Activity in Response to Affective Stimuli," *Psychological Science,* vol. 18, no. 5 (2007), http://www.scn.ucla.edu/pdf/AL(2007).pdf.

4   Sayadaw U. Pandita, "What Is Vipassana Meditation and How Do You Practice It?" *Lion's Roar,* May 3, 2018, https://www.lionsroar.com/how-to-practice-vipassana-insight-meditation.

5   Bruce D. Schneider, *Energy Leadership: Transforming Your Workplace and Your Life from the Core* (Hoboken, NJ: John Wiley & Sons, 2008), 132.

6   Ibid., 151.

**Chapter 16 – Cosmic Coach Conversations**

1   Bruce D. Schneider, Institute for Professional Excellence in Coaching, *Unconventional Wisdom: A Collection of Principles, Aphorisms, and Quotes from the Teachings of the Institute for Professional Excellence in Coaching* (2009), 22.

2   Wayne W. Dyer, EdD. "Contemplate to Create," drwaynedyer.com (accessed April 13, 2019), https://www.drwaynedyer.com/blog/contemplate-to-create/.

**Chapter 17 - Treasure Found**

1   Laura Koniver, "Sacral Chakra Support: 5 tips for Instant Relief," Intuition Physician, June 16, 2014, http://www.intuition-physician.com/sacral-chakra-support.

2   A Facebook video featuring Laura Koniver (accessed April 13, 2019), https://www.facebook.com/watch/?v=901406846589687.

**Chapter 18 – Gem Lessons**

1   Toni Morrison, Speech to the Ohio Arts Council, 1981, Apnews.com, https://www.apnews.com/7631ae6223894408b4fca49ab1874f4f.

2   Eckhart Tolle and OverDrive Inc., *The Power of Now: A Guide to Spiritual Enlightenment* (Novato, CA: New World Library, 2010), 49.

3   Daniel J Siegel, M.D., *Aware: The Science and Practice of Presence* (New York: Penguin Publishing Group, 2018), 19.

4   Pema Chodron, *When Things Fall Apart: Heart Advice for Difficult Times* (Boulder, CO: Shambhala Publications, 2000), 85.

5   Team Tony, "The 2-Millimeter Rule: How Small Changes Can Bring Massive Results," Tony Robbins (accessed April 13, 2019), https://www.tonyrobbins.com/stories/business-mastery/2-millimeter-rule/.

# ABOUT THE AUTHOR

 **Lana Williams,** founder of Look With Me™ Coaching, has a dream to be part of the shift in this life away from self-abandonment and toward the discovery of unconditional love, joy, and purpose. She is already personally experiencing the pleasure of the beautiful ripple effect that occurs when we radiate that love and light outward to others. Having hung up her physician's white coat, she is currently appreciating this chapter in her life as a life and relationship transformation coach. Lana is an emerging voice in the field of self-development and inspiration. She started in fertility coaching and later served as the head community coach for a national matchmaking company. Wherever this coaching path takes her is where you'll find her. When she is not immersed in all things coaching, she can also be found enjoying live music, nature, animals, girlfriend spa days, and quality playtime with her husband.

Made in the USA
Las Vegas, NV
28 September 2021

31271358R00154